Repairs at Sea

Repairs
at
Sea

The Seamanship Series

Nigel Calder

International Marine Publishing Company
Camden, Maine 04843

Published by International Marine Publishing Co.,
    a division of Highmark Publishing Ltd.,
    21 Elm Street, Camden, Maine 04843.

Typeset by Camden Type 'n Graphics, Camden, ME
Printed and bound by Bookcrafters, Chelsea, MI

Line Illustrations by Rod McCormick
Production Coordinator: Janet Robbins

10 9 8 7 6 5 4 3 2 1

Library of Congress Cataloging-in-Publication Data

Calder, Nigel.
    Repairs at sea.

    Includes index.
    1. Yachts and yachting—Maintenance and repair.
2. Boats and boating—Maintenance and repair.   I. Title.
VM331.C28   1988   623.8'223'0288   87-26260
ISBN 0-87742-249-4

To Ray:
a good friend and shipmate,
and the ultimate test of a piece of equipment!

Contents

Quick Reference Charts

Preface

This book is dedicated to the average mortal who gets careless, makes mistakes, or is just downright unlucky. It is hoped the reader may find something in this slim volume that will show up some weakness of maintenance and enable him or her to nip a potential crisis in the bud. Failing this, if the gods strike, then my objective is to show how to undertake immediate damage control and turn a looming disaster into a minor (though perhaps costly) irritation, by making . . . repairs at sea.

Thankfully, while I have had my fair share of mishaps, much of this book is based on other people's experiences rather than my own! In the past six months, as my family has sailed the Bahamas, the Dominican Republic, Puerto Rico, the Virgin Islands, and down through the West Indies, at each anchorage I have gone out seeking maritime horror stories. I must thank all those boat owners who have good humoredly put up with my ghoulish interest in their individual calamities.

My thanks go also to: AC Spark Plug; Champion Spark Plug Company; Edson International; ITT/Jabsco; Lucas/CAV Ltd.; Mercury Outboards; OMC; Pleasure-Craft Marine (PCM); Perkins Engines Ltd.; Schaefer Marine; Seagull Outboards; Sta-Lok Terminals; and Wilcox Crittenden. I wish to thank Henry Keene of Edson International for reviewing Chapter 2.

The illustrations on pages 51, 53, 54, 55, 57, 59, 60, 61, 63, 64, and 67 were provided by Edson International.

The illustrations on pages 135, 136, 138, 139, 146, 147, 150, 153, and 156 are reproduced from *Car Care,* published by the Automobile Association (UK), Basingstoke, England.

Tom Baker reviewed the manuscript with great care and raised a mass of detailed questions that cleared up many ambiguities. Jonathan Eaton at International Marine has guided the project from the start through long-distance telephone calls to Louisiana, then to Grenada, and later to Montana! To both of them I owe a considerable debt. Any mistakes remaining are solely mine.

Nigel Calder
Montana
August 1987

Introduction

This book is about how to deal with problems *after* they have arisen, not about routine maintenance. But let me be absolutely clear: prevention is a hundred times better than a cure.

The majority of equipment failures at sea (or anywhere else for that matter) do not come out of a clear blue sky. As often as not, they arise out of preexisting problems of which we are already aware. I am reminded yet again of a galvanized T that I fitted to the bronze water intake seacock on our boat six years ago. I could not lay my hands on a bronze T of the right size at the time, as is so often the case when one examines how crises develop. I am fully aware that electrolysis could be eating out the insides of the T and that it could *sink our boat*. And yet for six years I have stubbornly pushed the thought to the back of my mind because there is a mess of plastic plumbing that will have to be cut away in order to change it.

I'll bet there isn't a single reader who doesn't have at least one or two nagging problems that he plans to fix "later." Remember that Murphy's Law applies here with a vengeance. If something is going to fail, it will do so on a black, squally night close to a lee shore. Far easier to fix things in the calm and comfort of your mooring. By doing so, you may very well make the rest of this book unnecessary. Nothing would make me happier.

If you do get caught short at sea, this book has some suggestions on how to handle various rigging and equipment failures, and some basic steps for dealing with engines that won't run. My objective is not necessarily to show you how to fix the problem, but to explain how to get the boat and crew to a safe haven where proper repairs can be carried out.

The body of this book examines various troubleshooting and emergency repair procedures in some depth. Throughout the book are a number of quick reference summary charts for rapid access in an emergency situation.

When faced with a problem at sea, particularly a sudden emergency, having the right attitude is critical. This is especially true for the captain. Panic and confusion, a lot of running around and shouting, will be instantly communicated to the crew and will destroy any possibility of a coherent and reasoned response to the situation. Nine times out of ten, things are not as bad as they seem. If the mast just fell over the side, so what? No one is hurt, waves are not breaking over the boat, there are no rocks nearby, there is no danger of sinking. There is time to take a breather and work out the best way to handle matters.

Finally, remember that all mechanical things (and not just engines, but also pumps, blocks and tackles, rigging purchases, and the like) operate in strict accordance with *logical* principles. Troubleshooting any mechanical difficulty is therefore little more than *the application of logic* to the situation. This logic must be informed by an understanding of the mechanical process in question, but such understanding generally is easily acquired. What is much harder is to be able to step back from the problem and work one's way through it in a methodical fashion.

Knowledge itself, without a structured approach, can be positively damaging. Confronted with troubles resembling something I have already encountered, I have many a time jumped to the wrong conclusion, rushed in, and created myself a whole lot of unnecessary work. The essence of a troubleshooter is to stay cool, stay calm, be logical, and *don't take short cuts.*

With these thoughts in mind, let us take a look at some problems that may develop and procedures to deal with them.

1

Dealing with Rigging Failures

The majority of rigging failures occur at the attachment point of stays and shrouds to a mast or boat. All rigging flexes constantly as a boat works. If clevis pins and toggles become corroded and freeze up in their sockets, the wire terminals are no longer free to pivot as the rigging flexes. The wire ends, terminals, turnbuckles (rigging screws), tangs, and chainplates then absorb flexing loads for which they are not designed, become work hardened, and come to grief.

Improper installation is also a major cause of rigging failures. On a recent inspection of boats in a large marina, I found a staggering 30 percent of the headstays fitted without toggles. The major offenders were retrofitted foil-type roller-reefing headstays that had been tacked directly to the stemhead.

Although it is rarely done, even with a hanked-on headsail it is advisable to fit a toggle at the *upper* end of the headstay as well as the lower end. This helps to absorb the sideways loading caused by headstay sag. The upper toggle becomes essential with a roller-reefing headsail. When the sail is reefed, no matter how tightly the headstay is set up, the combined weight of the sail and reefing apparatus will set the headstay flexing in all directions if the boat is pitching. Without lower *and upper* toggles it is likely to be only a matter of time before the rig comes tumbling down.

Before a complete rigging failure occurs, however, there are often warnings. Welded fittings are prone to crack at the welds; swaged terminals will develop stress cracks at the

1

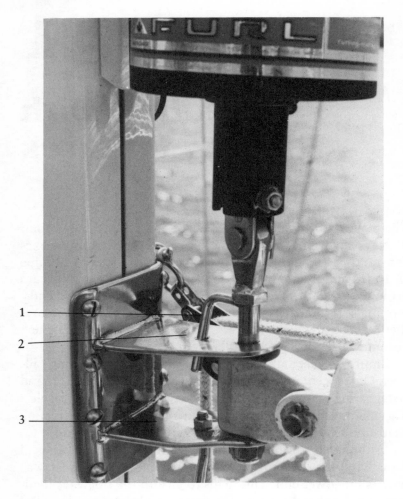

Mainsail roller-furling gear. This is a brand-new boat, but already the pin (1) is bending. Soon its weld will break and the whole rig will unwind uncontrollably. The two gooseneck retaining plates (2 and 3) are also flexing upward. In time these welds will crack and the whole boom and sail assembly will come loose.

swage; and wire rope will generally begin to "strand" (loose strands break and stick out) before complete failure. More insidious is electrolysis or galvanic action, especially on stain-

This is the backstay fitting on an otherwise beautifully equipped Gulfstar 50. Several other swages are in almost as bad condition. Some $20,000 of rig, not to mention the boat and perhaps the lives of the crew, are at risk.

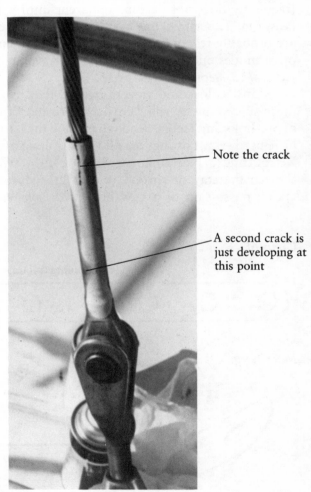

Note the crack

A second crack is just developing at this point

less steel fittings. Stainless steel depends on a regular supply of oxygen to maintain its surface resistance to corrosion. *Any stainless fitting that is either immersed in stagnant water (for example, a centerboard hinge pin) or allowed to trap stagnant water inside itself (for example, many lower wire terminals) is likely to corrode, sometimes at an alarming rate.* Stainless steel swage fittings and barrel-type turnbuckles (rigging screws) are notorious for this, especially in the tropics, the biggest problem being that there is no external evidence of the corrosion and it frequently does not become apparent until a stay or shroud fails. One expert reckons that "trapped puddles of salt water are probably responsible for more rigging failures than all the other modes put together" (Donal D. Kavanagh. *Ocean Navigator* #15, Sept/Oct 1987, p. 59).

Many sailors and riggers believe that swage fittings are more susceptible to this "crevice corrosion" than Norsemans or Sta-Loks and recommend retrofitting the latter, while others have used swage fittings for 10 years or longer without failure. Retrofitting a Norseman or Sta-Lok to a swaged wire will shorten the stay or shroud, so the procedure is not easy. If taking possession of a new boat with swage fittings on the

Chainplate.

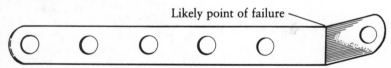

Mast tang.

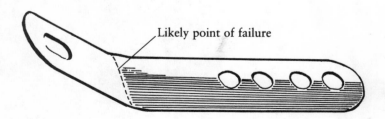

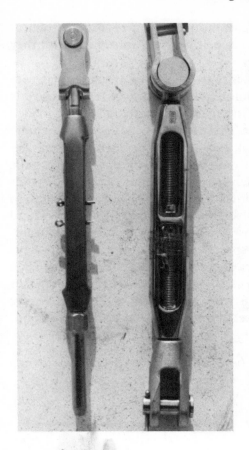

Toggle

The lower ends of these two turnbuckles offer two views of a toggle
fitting, which can swivel and therefore flex in two directions, around
the clevis pin and around the toggle.
With a toggle and fork at the chainplate end, a swage (right) or fork
terminal (left) works well at the upper end of the turnbuckle.

A correctly
rigged turn-
buckle and
chainplate. The
toggle and fork
allow the rig-
ging to flex in
any direction
without stress.

lower ends of the rigging, it is an excellent idea to gently heat all the lower terminals and melt beeswax into them until they are completely filled.

Jaw fittings are weaker than eye fittings when used as wire terminals. The slightest misalignment of the jaw will cause one side to take all the load. In time cracks develop and the loaded side of the jaw breaks off. These fittings need careful watching.

Spreaders rarely break except when wooden spreaders become rotten. In most instances, failure is due to either the spreader becoming detached from the mast, or else the outboard end riding up or down its shroud, causing the shroud to collapse inwards. In this case the spreader may then buckle and its attachment to the mast is almost certain to break as well.

Rigging should be inspected regularly for any telltale signs of trouble. We carry a set of crack detection dye spray cans on board and annually check all welds and wire terminals for hairline cracks. The dye will expose cracks invisible to the naked eye. It comes in a set of three cans—a cleaner, penetrant,

Rotten bobstay chain. The chain has stretched and the whole bowsprit is breaking loose from the boat.

Crack detection kit.

and developer. The instructions are clearly printed on the cans. Cost is $30 to $40, which is nothing compared with the cost of a rig. The dye can be obtained from engineering supply houses or, at a higher price, from automobile parts stores.

Unloading a Rig

Let's assume we get unlucky and there goes a shroud or stay (the collapse of a spreader should be treated as a case of the loss of the shroud it supports). The mast is in immediate danger but fast action can often save it.

Regardless of the point of sail at the time of failure, the loss of the backstay puts the rig in the most danger. Let fly the headsail sheet, put the helm down, and let the boat round up into the wind as quickly as possible. Then center the main boom on the traveler and winch in the mainsheet and vang (kicking strap) hard. With a little luck, the mainsail leech will hold the masthead until the topping lift or a spare halyard can be used to make temporary repairs. If the boat has running backstays, both should be set up tight.

Faced with the loss of a shroud, a rapid tack or jibe will transfer the load to the opposite shroud and allow repairs to be made. If the headstay parts, the luff of the headsail will provide support until a replacement is rigged. Meanwhile, the boat should be run off downwind to put the mast loads on the backstay.

Roller-Reefing Headsails

Roller-reefing headsails create special problems. There are essentially two varieties: those mounted independently of the headstay (known as roller-furling), and those mounted on a foil on the headstay. If the headstay fails on the former, the luff of the sail will support the masthead. The furling drum on a foil-mounted sail, however, is generally attached to the stay itself (for example, with a bolt through a turnbuckle). If the stay fails *below* or *at* the attachment point of the drum, the mast will have no support forward and the boat must be run off downwind as fast as possible to unload the mast. If the stay fails *above* the drum, the luff of the sail will support the mast. On boats with headstay-mounted roller reefing, it is an excellent practice always to keep a spare spinnaker topping lift set up tight to the stemhead, forward of the sail, if at all possible. In the event the gear fails, an emergency stay is already rigged. Alternatively, a separate attachment can be made from the base of the furling drum to the stemhead.

ROLLER-REEFING INSTALLATIONS

An arrangement that allows only sideways flexing.

This configuration allows only fore-and-aft flexing.

Correctly installed head-stay and roller-reefing gear.

Excellent headstay hard-ware.

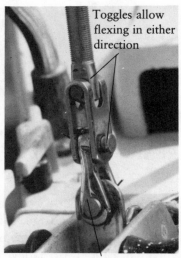

Toggles allow flexing in either direction

Toggles allow flexing in either direction

This toggle is an unnecessary extra

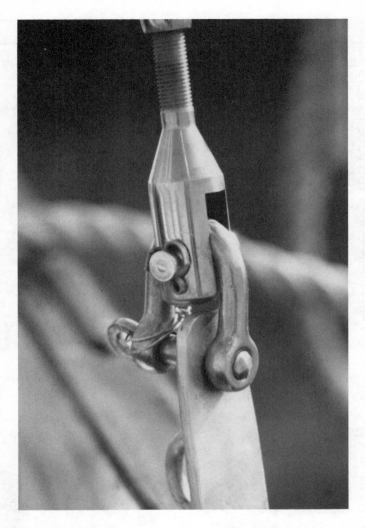

Use of a shackle as a temporary toggle. The shackle pin has been correctly lashed with seizing wire.

Should a roller-reefing rig fail below the drum, going forward with the headstay, sail, foil, and drum flogging around will be extremely dangerous. Generally, the furling line is led through a block or padeye close to the stemhead; hauling in this line should bring things back under control. After a temporary stay has been rigged (see below), the boltrope of the sail will have to be slid out of the foil to get the sail down, but this can only be done if the sail is completely unfurled. It may prove necessary to motor around in circles, working the furling line and sheets. If the sail is undamaged it can be reset with its foot fastened to the stemhead and its luff flying free (that is, without hanks).

Headsail roller-furling gear. This headstay has no toggle, but this is permissible because headsail sag affects only the headsail luff wire and mounting, which is adequately toggled.

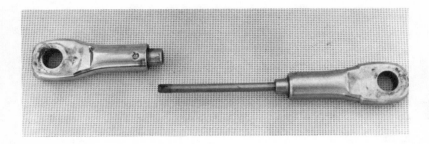

This piece was used to raise an expensive roller-furling rig off the foredeck. As the rig was unwound and rewound, the rod twisted until it failed (after only a few months' use). The rig (sail, foil, and furling drum) came loose and flailed around, endangering life and limb. This fitting was on the same boat as the one pictured on page 2!

Restoring a Rig

Alternative Stays and Shrouds

Between the topping lift, spinnaker pole topping lifts, and spare halyards, there are almost always two or three lines available to provide temporary support to a masthead. These can be sheeted off to chainplates or any other available strong point and winched in tight. The further out from the base of the mast they are attached, the more support they will provide. Low-stretch Dacron or wire halyards are eminently suitable; nylon anchor line is of little use due to its stretch.

Attaching Rope to Wire

Now comes the task of repairing the rigging. Assuming one is not an experienced rigger, attaching rope to a wire cable is at best a temporary measure. The knot to use is a double sheet bend (also called a double becket hitch) or a rolling hitch. A double sheet bend requires a loop to be formed in the end of the cable, which is easier said than done in wire sizes of 1/4 inch and up (see below). A rolling hitch requires a cable clamp below the knot or it will slip off. Vise-Grips ("mole wrenches") set up tightly and taped shut will do in a pinch.

Double sheet bend.

Rolling hitch.

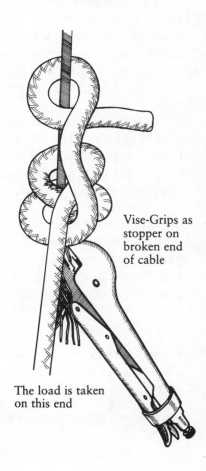

Vise-Grips as stopper on broken end of cable

The load is taken on this end

Making Loops in Broken Wire Rope

Any serious cruiser should carry one or two thimbles and some cable, bulldog, or Crosby clamps to make more permanent repairs. These clamps should be matched to the size of the boat's rigging (for example, 1/4-inch clamps for 1/4-inch wire rope). A broken wire is wrapped around a thimble and fastened with the clamps. A minimum of two is needed, and three are better, spaced to cover a span of at least 6 inches. The U of the clamp goes over the bitter (broken) end of the cable, with the clamp plate ("saddle") over the standing (loaded) part.

Cable clamps are either galvanized mild steel or stainless steel. In the smaller sizes (up to 3/8 inch), galvanized clamps are prone to shearing off when done up tightly, so it is better to use stainless steel. Stainless clamps, however, are prone to slipping and so *must be done up tightly*. Cable clamps should be periodically checked and retightened during the first day or so after being installed.

Larger wire sizes are hard to wrap around a thimble. The trick is to make a large loop, put a cable clamp around loosely, insert the thimble, and then knock the clamp down toward the thimble (or pull the bitter end of the cable through the clamp) until the cable has snugged up tightly around the thimble.

In an emergency, if no clamps are available and the boat has wheel steering with cable drive, two or three clamps will probably be found on each side of the cable adjusters. It may be possible to borrow one from each adjuster if they are the right size. They cannot be used if they are too small, but oversized clamps will work if pulled up tightly.

Correct installation of cable clamps.

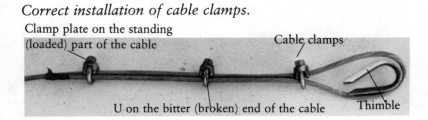

Clamp plate on the standing (loaded) part of the cable

Cable clamps

U on the bitter (broken) end of the cable

Thimble

If no cable clamps are available in a really tight spot, a pair of Vise-Grips can be used above a thimble. The Vise-Grips will need to be firmly set and taped closed (so that they will not spring apart at the wrong time), and a strong lashing must be put on the cable between the thimble and grips.

If no thimbles are on board, a loop will have to be made in the end of the wire without one, but this will lead to kinking of the cable under load, considerably reducing its strength. With prior practice, you can use a Flemish splice to make a strong loop without tools or hardware. The procedure is outlined on pages 25–29.

Wire rope that is beginning to strand but has not yet broken should have another length clamped alongside, above and below the weak spot. The U of the clamp should be put on the new wire, the saddle over the old wire. It is also possible to lengthen broken wire by clamping another piece alongside, but this makes a weak joint prone to slipping and failure. It is far better to form an eye as described above.

If a shroud or stay has parted up the mast and there is any way of turning it end for end so that the broken piece is at deck level, this should be done. It will make working on it so much easier.

Tensioning Emergency Stays and Shrouds

Make up a "handy billy," connected between the thimble and the chainplate, to winch the rig up tight. A handy billy is two multiple blocks with a line rove through. The blocks on the mainsheet system probably will suffice if others are not available. The line pull is multiplied by the number of ropes at the *moving* block—that is, the block that is being pulled down.

In the absence of suitable blocks, two shackles or thimbles with a number of turns of 1/4-inch or 3/8-inch line run through can be worked up tight and will take a great deal of strain. Tension can be increased by sticking a screwdriver or spike through the turns and twisting it around and around, creating a "Spanish windlass." The end of the screwdriver must then be tied off securely to stop it from undoing itself.

Front and back views of a handy billy.

Moving block
(line pull
multiplied by 4)

Multiple wraps of ¹/₄-inch line through two shackles.

Spanish windlass using a winch handle. The "windlass" must be tied off when tight.

Substituting for Broken Tangs

When a tang fails, loop an emergency stay or shroud around the mast. To keep it from slipping down, run the loop above a spreader, hold it up with a spare halyard, or lash shackles or blocks to the mast to which it can be attached. You may need to put a groove or dent in the mast under the lashing to stop it from slipping. The mainsail track will no longer be usable above the new shroud or stay, reducing the area of main that can be set.

Repairing Spreaders

A spreader increases the shroud's mechanical efficiency by increasing the angle between a shroud and the mast it supports. The taller a mast, the more important the spreaders. The mast

Emergency stay hooked over spreaders. Spreader sockets must be strong enough to take the load.

Emergency stay run through a block lashed to the mast. The mast may need grooving or denting at point A to prevent the block from slipping. Alternatively, a halyard attached to the lashing at this point could be used to hold it up.

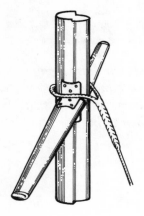

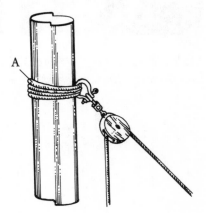

is liable to crumple or break above a failed spreader, which in turn would cause the loss of the headstay and backstay(s) and put the whole mast at risk.

A spreader must *bisect the angle it imparts to its shroud.* All the stresses are then concentrated as a compression load directed toward the mast. The more grossly a spreader violates this rule, the greater the flexing loads and the more likely it is to fail. If a spreader tip slips up or down its shroud, it needs to be knocked back into position and then locked with cable clamps around the shroud above and below the spreader. If no

Correct spreader installation. All loads are compression loads directly transmitted to the mast.

No spreaders. This configuration gives very little support to the masthead because of the narrow angles between shrouds and mast. The taller the mast, the narrower the angles.

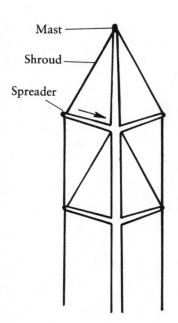

Mast ——
Shroud ——
Spreader

clamps are available, a tight figure-eight lashing will have to suffice.

A spreader may also come under unfair loads if the rigging is slack on the lee side, allowing the spreader to pump backward and forward when the boat is beating into the seas, or if there are no intermediate backstays and the mainsail is let out until it bears on the spreader when running downwind. In both instances if the spreader is rigidly mounted to the mast it is likely to become fatigued at its socket or bent.

Wooden spreaders, especially if varnished and in the tropics, are frequently stripped bare on their upper surfaces by the sun. Water then enters the wood grain and rot sets in. It can take as little as six months to destroy a spreader this way.

Spreader tip slipping up shroud. The load on the spreader resolves itself into an inward force and a downward force, tending to flex and break the spreader.

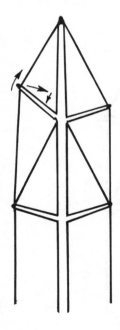

RIGGING FAILURES: QUICK REFERENCE

Instant Action

Faced with the loss of a stay, shroud, or spreader, unload the rig as fast as possible as follows:

- Headstay: Let fly the headsail sheet but leave headsail up. Run off
  (p. 8)   downwind to put mast loads on the backstay(s).
- Backstay: Let fly the headsail and mainsail sheets; come up into
  (p. 8)   the wind with the mainsail still set, center the boom,
              and winch down the vang (kicking strap).
- Shrouds: Tack or jibe to place the broken shroud on the lee side.
  (p. 8)
- Spreader: Treat it as the loss of the shroud it supports.

Immediate Repairs

Keep the boat from rolling and pitching as far as possible.

- Stays: Use a spare halyard to make temporary repairs. Winch
  (p. 12)   it up tight.
- Shrouds: Keep the load off the relevant shroud until a replace-
  (p. 12)   ment can be jury rigged.

Jury Rigging

1. Broken wire rope: Form a loop in the end (pp. 12–15). Tack on a handy billy (p. 15) and winch it up tight.
2. Broken tangs: Loop a replacement stay or shroud around the mast above a spreader, or support as outlined on p. 18, and then proceed as in (1) above.
3. Broken turnbuckle: Discard and replace. If no spare, proceed as in (1) above.
4. Broken chainplate: Find an alternative point of attachment.
5. Collapsed spreader: see pp. 18–22.

A broken spreader base fitting will need some improvised fastenings or lashings—it is difficult to be specific given the variety of spreaders and potential breaks. Just bear in mind that the spreader is under the most pressure to slip *down* the mast. If butted up squarely on the mast, it is under very little pressure to move fore and aft.

If a broken or buckled spreader cannot be straightened and braced with splints, any straight-grained, knot-free piece of wood of approximately the same cross section and length as the spreader can be pressed into service as a temporary replacement. Cut a slot in the outboard end to prevent the shroud from jumping out, then tack a strip of tin from a hacked-up can around the end of the emergency spreader and into the slot to stop the shroud from cutting into or splitting it. The shroud will also need lashing around the spreader end to stop it from slipping.

If a spreader cannot be repaired or replaced, retension the shrouds without it. This will greatly reduce the athwartship support to the mast (and the taller the mast, the greater the loss of support), but it is considerably better than nothing at all.

Emergency Rigging Kit

Sta-Lok Terminals and Norseman Marine manufacture wire terminals that can be fitted without the use of jigs, fixtures, swaging tools, or any other specialized equipment. We always carry a range of sizes on board, plus one length of wire as long as the longest stay on our boat. This gives us the capability to renew any shroud or stay at sea.

Although almost all standing rigging is made up from 1×19 stainless steel wire, it is in some ways preferable to carry 7×19 wire in the emergency rigging kit. This is more flexible, easier to form into eyes, and can be used for repairs to steering cables. However, it will be necessary to carry some 7×19 inserts (bushings) for any Norseman or Sta-Lok terminals, as well as the more common 1×19 bushings, as the two are not the same. A good all-around cable size to carry is 1/4-inch. Those with more extensive emergency rigging kits should also consider carrying a ¼-inch Nicopress kit, which will enable secure eyes to be made up rapidly. Wrenches, Vise-Grips, needlenose pliers, hammer, and punches (to knock out frozen clevis pins) are good candidates for the rigging kit.

Sta-Lok fittings. The threaded nut slides up the cable, and the outer wires are unlaid (1). A bushing is slid up the core cable (2). A washer is slipped into the end terminal (3), and the terminal and nut are firmly screwed together (4).

Terminal   Washer   Bushing   Nut

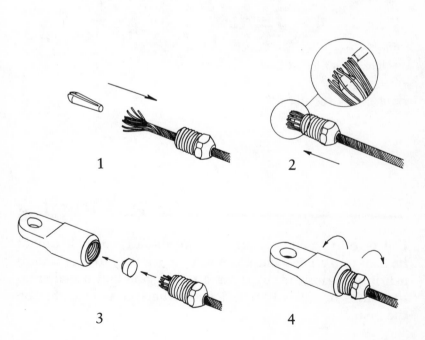

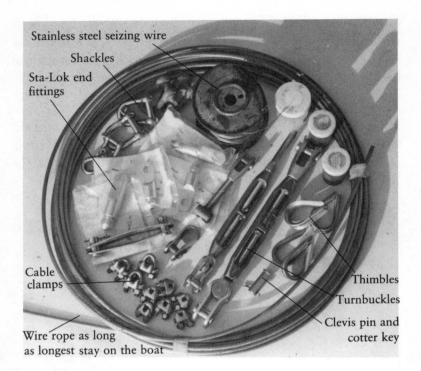

Emergency rigging kit.

Rod Rigging

Failed rod rigging is virtually impossible to repair. It cannot be bent into an eye and it is much too slippery to give clamps a firm grip. Instead, bypass the rod rigging and use alternative stays or shrouds rigged with whatever is available on the boat.

Flemish splice

It is possible to make an extremely strong eye in the end of a wire rope without the use of any tools. The method is fast and relatively simple *once the procedure is grasped*. However, it is not something to be learned in an emergency situation. The procedure was shown to me by Alan Tooley, a rigger out of Toronto, whom we met on his boat *Trident II* in the Dominican Republic.

1. Put a piece of tape around the cable to be spliced, approximately 18 to 24 inches back from the bitter (broken) end—the larger the wire, the farther back.
2. The outer layer of 1 × 19 cable (common rigging wire) has 12 strands. Take six strands next to each other and unlay them all the way back to the tape, keeping them all lined up side by side in their correct relationship. It helps if they are taped together after the first turn is unlaid.

Left: *Unlaying the first 6 strands.*
Right: *Weaving the first 6 strands back around the second 6 (with the core cable inside).*

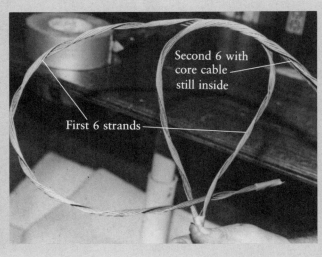

3. Do the same thing with the other six outer wires, but unlay them some 6 inches less than the first six.
4. Take the second six strands midway between the original tape mark and the point at which the core cable now emerges from them; take the first six strands at a similar point up from the original tape mark; bend them in toward each other to form an eye and hold them together.

The first 6 strands have been woven down to the base of the eye.

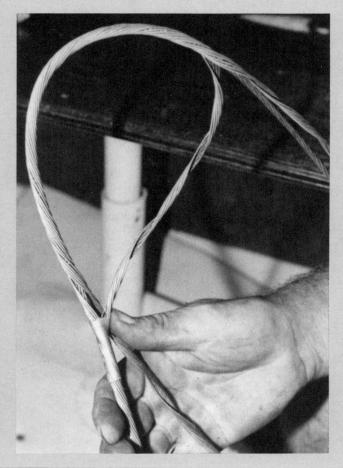

5. With a little experimentation you will find that the first six strands can be woven through the eye and laid back into the second six (which still have the core inside them at this point), working down to the base of the eye (that is, back toward the main, or standing, part of the cable) and reforming a *perfect* cable. When the main cable is reached there will be some 12 inches or so of the first six strands left. These are wrapped around the main cable and the end temporarily seized with a pair of Vise-Grips or substitute. *The key thing is at no point to force or deform the wire.* When done correctly, the first six strands will lay cleanly into the other wires. All that has to be done is to start in the right direction and to keep feeding the six strands through the eye until the main cable is reached. After that the six strands are gently worked around the main cable.

The second 6 strands with the core cable have been woven back down to the base of the eye. The last wrap is being made.

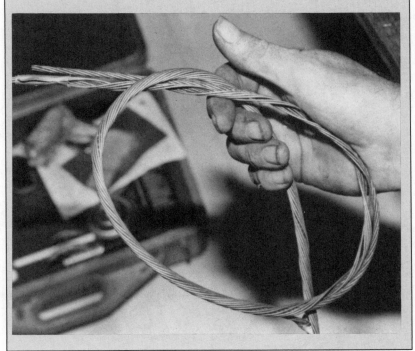

6. Now take the second six wires with the core cable inside and lay them into the first six, working around the eye in the opposite direction back to the main cable. There should now be a perfect cable in this direction. Once the main cable is reached, unlay the remaining 12 inches or so of the second six wires from the core and wrap them around the main cable alongside the first six, again seizing the end. This will leave the core cable sticking out at the base of the eye.

The eye is complete except that the wires have not yet been woven around the main part of the cable.

The first and second sets of wires have now been worked around the main cable.

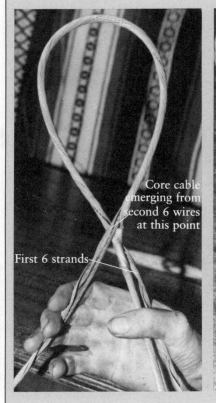

Core cable emerging from second 6 wires at this point

First 6 strands

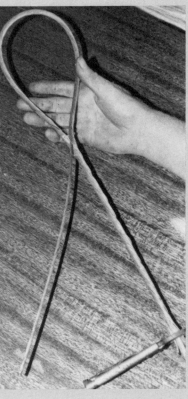

7. The core cable can now be unlaid (it has six wires wrapped around a center wire) and worked around the main cable alongside all the other wires, or it can just be seized up the main cable, although this is not as neat.

8. If a thimble is available, insert it in the eye, pinch the eye up tightly around it, and seize the splice up as tightly as possible.

The size of the eye can be varied according to need by varying the amount that the second six wires are unlaid in Step 3. For example, it can be made large enough to slip over a spar when jury rigging an emergency mast. For large eyes the tape will need to be placed farther back from the bitter end in Step 1.

The core cable unlaid.

The completed splice.

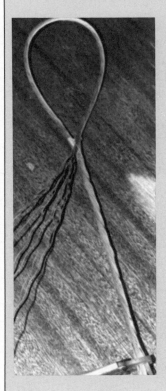

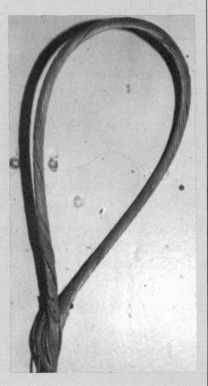

Loss of a Mast

The loss of a mast is almost always due to shroud or stay failure or collapse of a spreader, but sometimes it is caused by corrosion in aluminum masts or rot in wooden ones. Corrosion in aluminum is generally accompanied by blistering of painted surfaces and a telltale white powder (aluminum oxide). Rot in wood will reveal itself as dark areas under varnish or by a generally spongy feel.

The loss of a mast will be traumatic, but hardly ever seems to injure anyone or lead to the loss of the boat. There is generally no immediate emergency. The mast may break at the spreaders, or (if deck-stepped) the whole mast may go over the side. Keel-stepped masts are liable to crumple or break above the deck. Wooden masts have a certain amount of buoyancy. Aluminum spars will fill with water and sink unless they are foam filled.

The first reaction probably will be to crank the engine. *This is the last thing that should be done.* We have enough problems without adding a fouled propeller. In rough conditions when things seem at their very worst, it may even be possible to lie to the mast, using it as a sea anchor, while one collects one's thoughts.

Depending on the circumstances there might be three different objectives:

1. Cut the mess away as fast as possible.
2. Bring the mast and rigging under control and motor home.
3. Erect a jury rig and restore a limited sailing ability to the boat.

The decision hinges on distance offshore, possibility of rescue, immediate threat to the hull from the spars alongside, and the crew's initiative.

Cutting Away Rigging

The fastest way to clear rigging is with a good-sized pair of bolt cutters. Stainless steel wire is very resilient, and the trick in cutting it is to operate the bolt cutters with a sudden push rather than gradual pressure. A cold chisel with a good-sized hammer will always work its way through a wire cable if the cable is laid on a suitable block. An ax wielded with wild abandon will likewise cut wire, but this will do a tremendous amount of cosmetic damage if the deck or bulwarks serve as the chopping block. Sometimes a hacksaw is the only answer, but since stainless heats the blade and strips off teeth rapidly, a good supply of blades will be needed. The blade should be kept cool and lubricated with water. When cutting any cable, tape it firmly with electrician's or masking tape at the point of the cut to prevent stranding.

Most turnbuckles are mounted on toggles held to the chainplates with a clevis pin and cotter pin (also called a cotter key or split pin). Removing the cotter pins and knocking out the clevis pins will release the rigging a great deal faster than struggling to undo turnbuckles.

Try to recover your sails—you may need them for a jury rig—but weigh the danger to your boat of keeping a spar alongside. Retrieving waterlogged sails on jammed hanks and slides will be no easy task—it may prove necessary to cut the slide and hank lashings.

Rescuing a Mast

A waterlogged mast tied alongside will make the boat extremely hard to steer under power. The mast will need to be lightened and its drag reduced by removing as much of the rigging as possible, and it should be lashed in such a way that it can be cut loose in a hurry if an emergency develops. Wooden spars with some buoyancy might be towed, but more than one boat has been holed by a mast crashing through its side. It will also be necessary to keep a constant watch for possible fouling of the propeller by the towline.

Jury Rigging

Jury rigging presents a real challenge. Before attempting anything, all members of the crew will need to don lifejackets and safety harnesses. In any kind of a sea without the pressure of the wind in the sails to stabilize it, a sailboat will have a tremendously uncomfortable motion, making it virtually impossible to maneuver around cumbersome lengths of spar. By increasing windage forward (for example, by tying a sail to the bow pulpit), it may be possible to head the boat more or less downwind and ease things a little.

Break Above the Spreaders.   If the mast has broken above the spreaders and the lower shrouds are still intact, it may only be necessary to clear away the broken section, rig a temporary forestay and backstay as outlined above, and continue sailing using a reefed main or storm trysail and a storm jib. If the whole mast is over the side things will not be so easy.

Recovering an Overboard Mast.   All hollow spars, both wood and aluminum, will fill with water unless they are foam-filled. In order to stand any chance of raising one, you must lift it by the head so that the water runs out. If any kind of a stump is left on the boat, a block should be attached to its top and a line run from a winch through the block to a point a little above the midpoint of the overboard mast. This will bring the masthead up, at the same time placing most of the weight of the mast on the winch. Once the mast is back on board, the problem becomes one of finding suitable points of leverage to erect it.

Staying and Sail Plans.   Any reasonable sail area demands a decent length of spar, but as one raises taller masts the handling problems rapidly multiply out of control. The more lines that are left to trail from the new mast, the greater your command over it and the greater the number of pulling and levering options. Once it is up, it must be held by its new stays in at least a tripod formation.

Before it is raised, however, a rough sail plan must be worked out so that appropriate halyards can be set in place at its head. With a reduced mast height, it should be possible to set a jib with its foot attached to the forward "stay" and its luff running along the deck. It will be sheeted off at its former head.

Raising a Mast.   It is possible to raise a mainmast without the use of a crane. Some years ago, we stepped our 50-foot, 800-pound mast (with the rigging attached) by following certain general principles. Let us first see how we did it.

We faced the situation illustrated in the accompanying diagram. If a line is attached to the head of the mast and placed on the winch at deck level, the force exerted by the winch will drag the mast along the deck with no lifting effect whatsoever. If, however, we run the line through the mizzen masthead and then through a block at the base of the mizzen and onto the cockpit winch, we begin to get a lifting component. The greater the angle of the line to the mainmast head, up to 90 degrees, the more of our effort will go into lifting and the less into dragging. If the attachment point is made down the spar it will improve the angle of pull. Don't attach the line below the balance point of the spar, however, or you will raise the wrong end.

The early part of the lifting process is the hardest because we are lifting the whole weight of the spar at a very poor angle of pull. As the spar comes up, the angle steadily improves, while at the same time more and more of the mast's weight is supported by the heel. To get things started, the head should be physically manhandled up as far as possible.

Jumper Struts.   All this is very well if we still have a mizzen mast standing or a substantial stub of broken mast, but what if we don't? In the absence of a lever, we must create one. The simplest and most effective means is to add a "jumper strut" to the spar to be hoisted. The closer to the pivot point (base of the spar) the jumper strut is positioned, the greater its leverage

A setup for raising a mainmast using the winches on the boat.

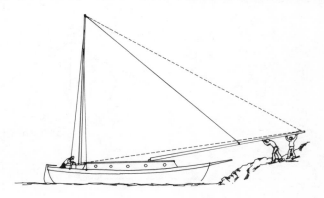

effect. The heavier the spar, however, the greater the compression load on the jumper and the stronger it will need to be.

By far the easiest way to form a jumper is to use the boom, if it is still intact, because it will already be well attached at its mast end. Its outboard end must be tied off securely to a point well up the mast using one of the old stays or a length of low-stretch Dacron (not nylon). A line is then run from the top of the mast, through a snatch block or a groove in the tip of the jumper, to whatever blocks are necessary to provide a fair lead to the biggest winch on the boat.

Bracing a Jumper Strut.   We still have a couple of engineering problems to be solved before hoisting. The jumper will want to pivot sideways, dropping the spar back on the deck. The way to brace it is to fit "diamond stays." A crossbar is

Jumper strut.

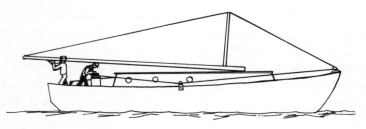

Jumper strut with diamond stays.

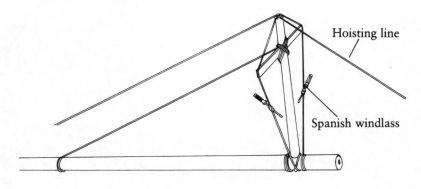

MAST FAILURES: QUICK REFERENCE

- Do not start the motor until all trailing lines are cleared.
- Determine whether to:
  1. Cut the mast loose and abandon it (p. 30).
  2. Salvage the mast and rigging (p. 31).
  3. Erect a jury rig (see below).
- Jury rigging:
  1. Recover the spar(s) and sail(s) and hoist on deck (pp. 31–32).
  2. Build a jumper strut if necessary (pp. 33–35).
  3. Provide the spar with athwartship support (pp. 35–39).
  4. Work out a jury-rigged sail plan and add all necessary stays and halyards *at this point*.
  5. Lift the masthead as high as possible (p. 33).
  6. Winch it up and secure.

---

fixed to the jumper, and wire or Dacron lines are run from the head of the jumper, over the ends of the crossbar, and down to the spar. The lines must be firmly fastened at both ends and set up taut, which can be done with a Spanish windlass: Place a screwdriver or length of rod through a loop in the lines, twisting until all is tight, and then tie off the screwdriver handle so that it cannot unwind.

Shrouds and Athwartship Bracing.　As the mast comes up, it is going to be very hard to keep the whole assembly from falling sideways; it is just not possible on a boat deck to get far enough out from the base of the mast to set up any effective "tailing" lines. If at all possible, set up wire shrouds to either side of and *at the same height as* the base of the mast. As the mast pivots up, these shrouds will maintain a constant tension. If this cannot be done, legs firmly lashed out to each bulwark in line with the base of the mast will provide the needed rigid bracing—a pair of spinnaker poles would be excellent. If the mast has broken up, two lengths lashed into an A frame will be far easier to hoist aloft than a single spar with sideways bracing.

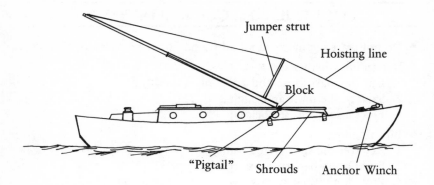

Jumper strut

Hoisting line

Block

"Pigtail"   Shrouds   Anchor Winch

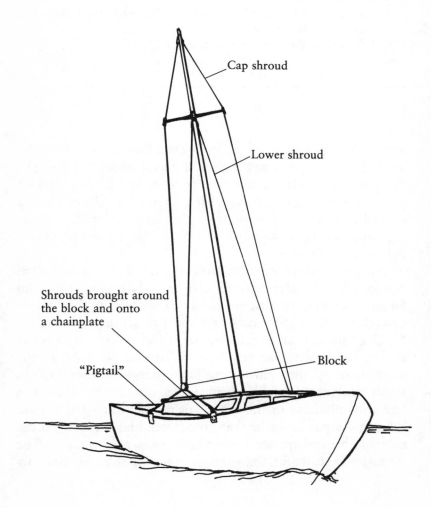

Cap shroud

Lower shroud

Shrouds brought around
the block and onto
a chainplate

"Pigtail"

Block

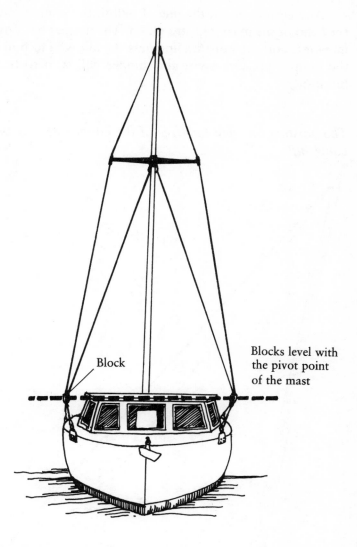

Block

Blocks level with
the pivot point
of the mast

Hoisting a spar with a jumper strut. Running the shrouds (both upper and lower, if desired) through a block and then to a chainplate provides more precise control as the mast is raised. A short line or "pigtail" from the block becket to an attachment point on deck can then be used to keep the block abreast and level with the pivot point of the mast.

At a certain point, the line of pull to the jumper and on to the head of the mast will straighten. The jumper has now done its work, and the hoisting line must be allowed to pull free of the jumper tip. Otherwise the jumper will start to become a hindrance.

The hoisting line will pull free of the jumper strut as the mast comes up.

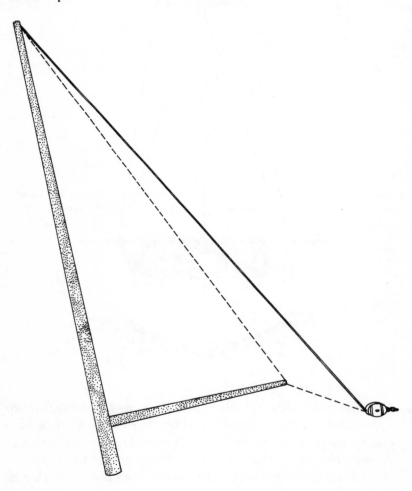

Alternative Methods.   While the method described has the jumper attached to the spar, it can, if necessary, be set up independently, just so long as its base is held firmly in place. For example, it can be wedged up against the front or back of the cabin, depending on which way the mast is being brought up. Two poles lashed together to form an A frame will provide a considerable amount of lateral stability.

Alternative jumper arrangement.

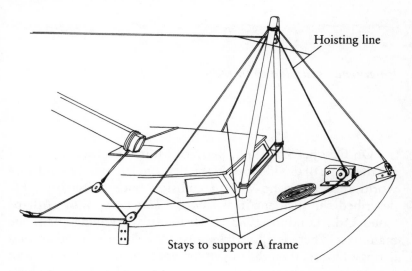

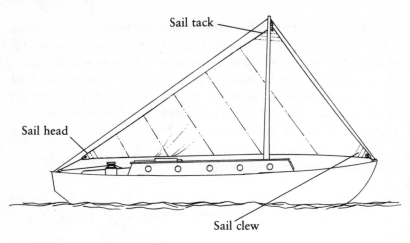

Sail tack

Sail head

Sail clew

Emergency sail plan with reduced mast height.

On October 20, 1968, Bernard Moitessier was approaching the Cape of Good Hope in the first singlehanded round-the-world race when he was in collision with a freighter. He described the incident in his book, *The Long Way* (Adlard Coles Ltd., London, 1983). "The stern's overhang snags the mainmast. There is a horrible noise. . . . The masthead shroud is ripped loose, then the upper spreader shroud. My guts twist into knots. The push on the mast makes *Joshua* heel, she luffs up towards the freighter . . . and wham!—the bowsprit is twisted 20 or 25 degrees to port. I am stunned." (*Joshua*'s bowsprit was made with 3-inch steel pipe with a second steel pipe inside it.)

Moitessier had rigged his boat in the first place using thimbles and cable clamps at the turnbuckles. Less than two hours later, the shrouds were repaired. "I did not have to climb the mast; only the lower cable clamps had slipped." He then rode out a gale, hove-to, and spent the hours thinking about his crippled bowsprit. Two days later, with the gale blown over and the seas subsiding, he rigged enough sail to steady his boat and went to work.

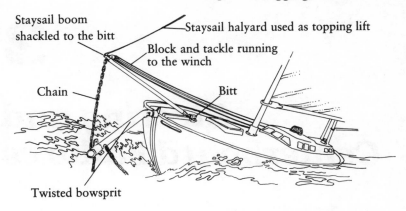

Moitessier's rig to straighten his bowsprit. (Redrawn from The Long Way. *Adlard Coles Ltd., 1983.)*

"I have prepared a large four-part block and tackle with the spare mizzen boom to increase the angle at which the block pulls. I hinge the spar to the forward bitt with a shackle. No, that won't do, another shackle is needed as a gimbal, so the spar can move both horizontally and vertically.

"Good, that should do the trick. The spare staysail halyard serves as a topping lift. The rig is strong, and swings easily off the starboard bow. I run a 3/8-inch chain from the tip of the bowsprit to the outer end of the spar and secure the tackle opposite, with the line running back to the big starboard Goiot winch.

"Incredible, the power of a tackle on a winch . . . I feel I'm going to start crying, it's so beautiful. . . . The bowsprit begins to straighten out, very, very slowly. I am wild with joy!"

Moitessier went on to sail 1½ times around the world without stopping. What a seaman, and what an exemplary way to handle this catastrophe! First, he took care of the immediate danger to his rig, and then he mulled the problem over at great length. Finally, he carefully applied basic mechanical principles to produce a force pulling at an angle that one would at first sight think impossible to achieve from within the confines of his boat. Here are all the ingredients to handle a crisis: fast action, patience, creative thinking, and methodical preparation. Should we ever need it, may just a little of his genius rub off on us all.

2

Steering and Centerboard Failures

Types of Rudders

There are two rudder types: transom mounted and shaft mounted. Transom rudders turn on hinge pins *(pintles)* bolted to the transom. The corresponding fittings on the rudder that slide over the pintle are known as *gudgeon*s. Gudgeons are firmly screwed or bolted to the rudder with metal straps.

Some transom-hung rudders are locked in place by inverting one of the pintles; they can only be lifted off by unbolting this pintle or its gudgeon. Others are simply dropped onto their pintles and retained with a nut threaded onto one of the pintles, or a pin through the pintle.

Shaft-mounted rudders have a central pipe (the *rudder stock)* to which is welded a metal framework (the *web)* around which the rudder is constructed, generally in fiberglass. Where the rudder stock enters the boat, there is a bearing, and at the top of the stock is another bearing. In order to prevent the entry of seawater around the stock, a seal (a *stuffing box* or *packing gland)* is placed on top of the lower bearing, or else the bearing and stock are contained inside a pipe, or *bearing tube*, which is sealed into the bottom of the boat. This bearing tube generally rises above water level to the second bearing. There may or may not be a stuffing box on top of the upper bearing, depending on its relationship to the boat's waterline.

Shaft rudders that project straight down from the bottom of the boat with no other support are known as *spade rudders*.

42

Sometimes a small *skeg* is built into the underbody of the boat, and a pintle and gudgeon-type pivot are added to the rudder halfway down its length. Some skegs are made large enough to come to the bottom of the rudder and a pintle and gudgeon are added at this point, known as the *heel bearing*.

Transom-mounted rudder.

This pintle and gudgeon is inverted to lock the rudder in place. To remove it, the pintle must be unbolted from the boat.

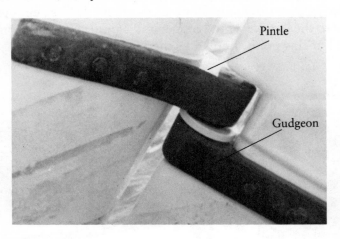

A more typical arrangement than that shown above, with a locking pin through the top pintle.

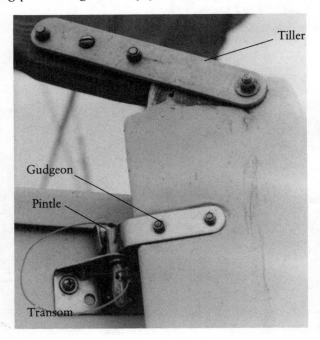

Types of Steering

Many transom-hung rudders and a few shaft-mounted ones are turned by a tiller, but the majority of boats over 25 feet today use a wheel. The drive from a wheel to the rudder is transmitted in a number of different ways.

Rack-and-Pinion or Worm Gears.   The wheel is mounted on a shaft that directly turns a rack-and-pinion or worm drive. If the rudder is raked at an angle, a universal joint will probably be installed on the drive shaft.

A spade rudder configuration.

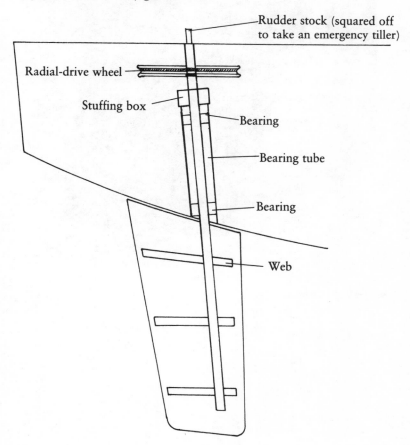

A half-skeg rudder.

A full-skeg rudder.

Cable Steering.   The steering wheel turns a sprocket, driving a length of chain. A wire cable is attached to each end of the chain, and the wires run around a variety of pulleys, or sheaves, to a fitting attached to the head of the rudder stock. This may be either a quadrant or a large pulley wheel, the latter arrangement being known as *radial drive* steering. When the steering wheel is turned, the quadrant or rudder wheel turns.

Pull-pull Steering.   This is essentially the same arrangement as in cable steering, with the exception that instead of running around sheaves, the wire cables are placed inside flexible conduits similar to those used in remote controls for outboard motors and engines. The steering wheel and rudder stock fittings remain the same as in a standard cable drive system.

Hydraulic Systems.   The steering wheel turns a hydraulic pump, which sends oil under pressure via hoses to a piston at the rudderhead. This turns the rudder via a lever arm. Sometimes the drive shaft on the pump is coupled directly to the steering wheel. At other times the steering wheel turns a sprocket, and an endless (circular) chain connects this sprocket to another on the pump drive shaft. Hydraulic steering is a powerful system found on larger boats.

Steering Failures

Tiller Units with Cheek Blocks

Any kind of a tiller-operated rudder is reasonably foolproof. If transom mounted, the likely points of failure are the tiller itself, its *cheek blocks* (the two wooden pads that hold the tiller in place at the rudderhead), or the pintles. The majority of tiller failures are due to poor grain in the wood. If a single piece of wood is used, the grain should run straight along its length when viewed from the side. It is better, however, to laminate a tiller from a number of thin, straight-grained strips of wood.

An oar or boathook can substitute for a broken tiller. It will probably have to be shaved down or padded to make a good fit where it enters the cheek blocks, and it will need a lashing to prevent if from slipping out. Bunk boards or hatch-covers tightly lashed in place will reinforce broken or cracked cheek blocks. The loads on both a tiller at the cheek blocks, and on the cheek blocks themselves, can be extremely high, so try to balance the boat as much as possible when using a jury rig. Little can be done to rectify broken pintles.

Cable Drive Units and Shaft-Hung Tiller Units

Shaft-hung rudders with tillers have a fitting clamped and keyed; clamped and pinned; or clamped and held with set screws (Allen screws) at the top of the rudder stock. The same three methods are used for fastening quadrants or wheel drives for cable and pull-pull steering (see drawing, page 54). Tremendous loads are concentrated at this point. *Any play is a sure sign of trouble to come and should be remedied at the earliest possible opportunity.*

Tiller installation showing a support ring to accept the weight of the rudder.

Support ring ——————

TILLER STEERING FAILURES: QUICK REFERENCE

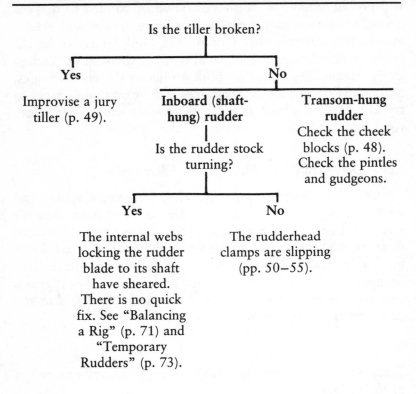

Is the tiller broken?

Yes   **No**

Improvise a jury
tiller (p. 49).

**Inboard (shaft-
hung) rudder**

Is the rudder stock
turning?

**Transom-hung
rudder**
Check the cheek
blocks (p. 48).
Check the pintles
and gudgeons.

Yes   **No**

The internal webs
locking the rudder
blade to its shaft
have sheared.
There is no quick
fix. See "Balancing
a Rig" (p. 71) and
"Temporary
Rudders" (p. 73).

The rudderhead
clamps are slipping
(pp. 50–55).

Slipping rudderheads.　Pinned rudderheads have a bolt or metal pin passing through the fitting and shaft. A sheared pin can be replaced with a bolt.

When set screws are used, these are threaded into the rudderhead fitting and either seat in a dimple drilled in the rudder stock or screw into a threaded hole in the rudder stock. The latter is much to be preferred since it locks the rudderhead to its stock, and if the boat has set screws seating in dimples it is well worth drilling out the dimples and tapping them to accept the set screws. Slipping set screws in dimples may hold up with

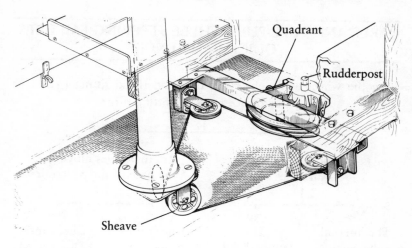

Quadrant

Rudderpost

Sheave

Above and below: *Cable drive with quadrant.*

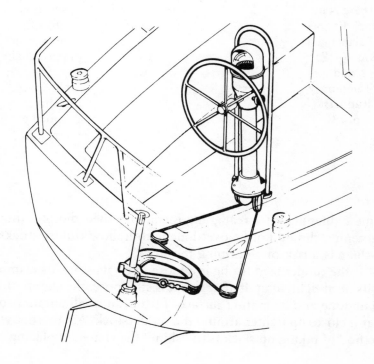

CABLE AND PULL-PULL WHEEL STEERING FAILURES: QUICK REFERENCE

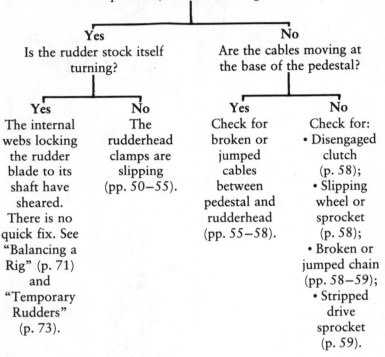

Turn the wheel while observing the rudderhead fitting (wheel or quadrant). Does the fitting turn?

Yes
Is the rudder stock itself turning?

Yes
The internal webs locking the rudder blade to its shaft have sheared. There is no quick fix. See "Balancing a Rig" (p. 71) and "Temporary Rudders" (p. 73).

No
The rudderhead clamps are slipping (pp. 50–55).

No
Are the cables moving at the base of the pedestal?

Yes
Check for broken or jumped cables between pedestal and rudderhead (pp. 55–58).

No
Check for:
• Disengaged clutch (p. 58);
• Slipping wheel or sprocket (p. 58);
• Broken or jumped chain (pp. 58–59);
• Stripped drive sprocket (p. 59).

some tightening after realigning them with their dimples (but tightening should not be overdone with hollow rudder stocks as there is a risk of deforming the stock).

If the rudderhead fitting is a loose fit on its stock its clamp bolts need tightening. If after this it is still loose, the clamp can be undone and its mating surfaces filed off a small amount so that it closes up tighter around the rudderstock. An alternative method of taking up slack is to "shim" the clamp by placing a thin piece of metal between the clamp and its shaft, and then doing the clamp back up. Cutting a strip of tin out of a sardine or soft drink can will be more than enough.

Keyed rudderheads have a groove cut in the rudder stock with a corresponding groove in the rudderhead fitting. A piece of square metal (the key) fits snugly in the grooves, so that the fitting and shaft turn as one. Clamps on the fitting prevent it from sliding up and down the shaft. In the marine environment it is essential that stainless steel keys be used throughout the steering system. Brass keys will lead to electrolysis and steering failure. With cable and pull-pull steering, the keyway and key are normally longer than the fitting in order to allow up and down adjustment of the quadrant or wheel to align it with its

Cable drive with radial-drive wheel.

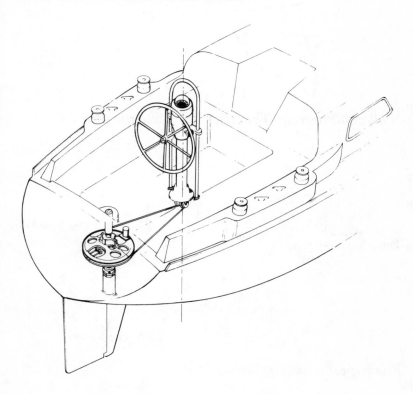

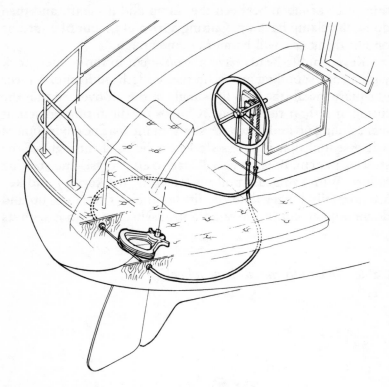

"Pull-pull" steering. The conduits replace the sheaves.

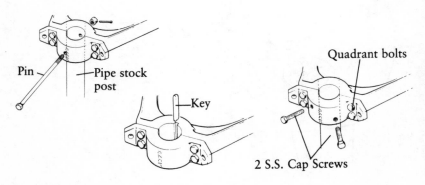

Rudderpost mounting arrangements.

drive cables. If the key becomes rounded and slips, it may just be possible to provide a fresh grip by raising or lowering the rudderhead fitting, or after loosening the clamp, by driving the key itself up or down a little in its slot.

Moving a quadrant or wheel will throw out the alignment of its cables, so any such adjustment must be limited. Note that spade-hung rudders with no pintles are held up in the boat at some point by a *load* or *thrust bearing*. Should this bearing be incorporated in the underside of the rudderhead fittings or held in place by it, *loosening the rudderhead may cause the rudder to drop out of the bottom of the boat!*

Jumping Cables. All cable-operated steering systems (with the exception of some pull-pull units) end up with sheaves leading the cables onto the quadrant or drive wheel. Several problems can cause the cables to jump off sheaves or the quadrant or wheel:

1. Misalignment: A straightedge set in the groove on one pulley should drop cleanly into the groove on the other. Alignment is adjusted by raising or lowering the rudderhead

Using a dowel for checking vertical alignment of a pull-pull steering system. The conduit must make its final approach (as through the bulkhead at right) at the precise level of the quadrant.

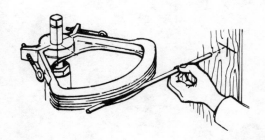

fitting on the keyway of a keyed fitting, or by adjusting the height and angle of the sheaves in a system using a rudderhead with a pin or set screws.

2. Loss of tension in the cables: If the steering wheel is locked up or lashed, it should not be possible to move the quadrant or rudder wheel by grasping it and applying torque. Tension is restored to a loose system by taking up on the adjusting bolts at the rudderhead, making sure that the locknuts are tightened afterward. The cables should be tightened just enough to remove any slack and no more—overtensioning will cause the system to bind up.

3. Loose sheaves: Loads on sheaves are high. In time, their fastenings may work loose, requiring refastening.

Broken Cables. What if a cable breaks? First, find out why. Probably one or more sheaves have frozen and the cable has frayed where it has been dragging over the pulley. If the emergency rigging repair kit contains a length of 1/4-inch 7 × 19 stainless steel wire and a Nicopress kit or appropriate cable

Steering system sheaves. Note that the baseplates are slotted to permit turning for alignment adjustment.

clamps, a new cable can be made up. Otherwise, by slackening off both cable adjusting nuts at the rudderhead, it should be possible to get enough slack to fasten the broken cable ends together with a cable clamp. If no clamp is onboard, one can be taken from the two that will probably be found on each side of the rudderhead attaching the cables to the cable adjusters.

Chain-to-cable connections, and (inset) a cable adjuster for quadrant and radial steering systems.

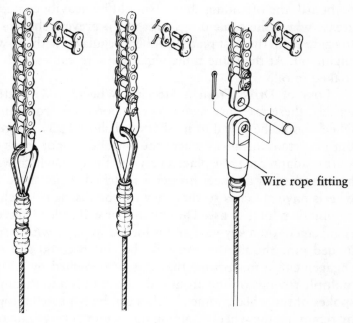

Wire rope fitting

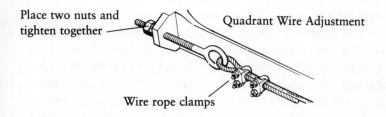

Place two nuts and tighten together

Quadrant Wire Adjustment

Wire rope clamps

For even partial steering to be restored, this splice must come between sheaves. Depending on the cable end fittings it may be possible to achieve this by turning the cable end for end, or else by playing with the adjusters. Take care, however, to see that the chain-to-cable adaptors are not pulled up onto the steering wheel sprocket (see below). Alternatively, it may be possible to clamp in a spare length of wire or Dacron line well back from the sheave on both sides, thus allowing limited movement.

Naturally any frozen sheaves will have to be freed up at the same time. Should this prove impossible, and if no spares are on board, the offending sheave should be heavily coated with grease where the cable drags over it. To prevent sheaves from freezing up in the first place, oil them regularly with 30-weight engine oil. At the same time, wipe the wire cables with a rag soaked in oil.

Loss of Drive From a Steering Wheel.   With steering wheels, there are once again several potential problems. The wheel should be keyed to its shaft and should give no trouble. But in certain instances where the wheel does not fit its shaft, a brass adapter may be placed between the two, which will not be as secure as a wheel properly matched to its shaft. Some wheels have clutches so that they can be disengaged when an automatic pilot is in use. The clutch unit will slide in and out of engagement on a keyway, and is locked in place with a spring-loaded pin. Should this pin fail, the clutch could slip out of engagement, a misfortune that can be remedied by wrapping multiple rovings of line around the back of it and through the spokes of the wheel. Some clutches can be bypassed altogether by removing the wheel retaining nut, sliding everything off the drive shaft, and replacing the wheel directly on the shaft. Be sure to replace the key in the keyway.

The wheel turns a sprocket that drives the chain. This chain is connected to the steering cables at both ends. Should there be a failure of the rudder stops (which, depending on the rudder configuration, are mounted on the transom, or in association with the quadrant or rudder wheel, etc., and serve to limit rudder movement), the chain-to-cable adapters may run up onto the sprocket and break off sprocket teeth. Sometimes the chain may come off the sprocket altogether.

Good, solid rudder stops are an essential piece of equipment with wheel steering, especially in boats making offshore cruises. Although stops are frequently built onto quadrants and radial drive wheels, it is far better to install them in the hull, independently of the steering system.

A wheel clutch disengages a wheel from the shaft when an autopilot or another wheel (with two-station steering) is in use. Adaptors make it possible to install wheels on otherwise incompatible shafts.

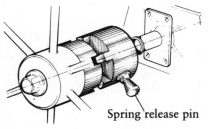

Spring release pin

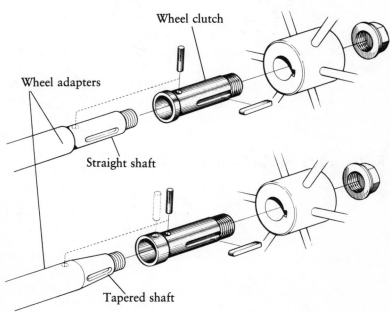

Wheel clutch

Wheel adapters

Straight shaft

Tapered shaft

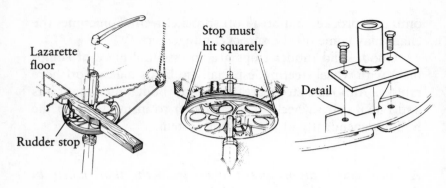

Lazarette
floor

Stop must
hit squarely

Detail

Rudder stop

Rudder stops mounted on a radial-drive wheel.

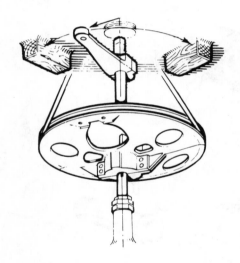

Rudder stops installed independently.

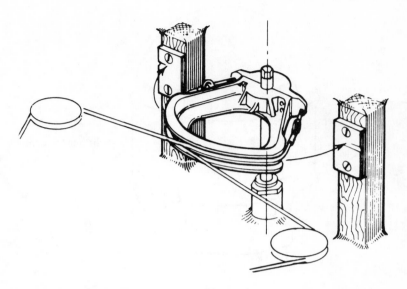

Rudder stops on quadrant steering.

Steering chains have a removable link at both ends and in the center. In the case of binnacle-mounted steering, access is gained by removing the compass from the top of the binnacle. To ensure accurate realignment when refitting the compass, mark the housing and binnacle base with three or four pieces of tape placed over the joint and then slit around the joint. After reassembly, the compass will have to be swung and readjusted.

The chain should be regularly lubricated. Number 30 weight engine oil will do just fine. Grease should not be used—it merely sits on the surface of the chain collecting dirt and fails to penetrate the links. If the pedestal has bronze shaft bushings these too should be oiled. Needle bearings, however (found on larger units), should be greased.

Binding Steering Wheels. If a wheel becomes hard to turn, *do not force it.* Check the brake first! If this is not the problem, check immediately for frozen sheaves or pull-pull cables, the latter being hard to test without first disconnecting them at

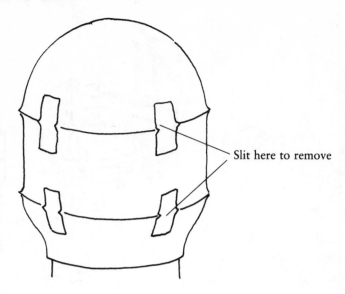

Slit here to remove

Using masking tape to realign a compass in its binnacle.

the rudderhead and then moving them in and out of their conduits. If the cables are stiff they should be removed from their conduits, cleaned, liberally greased—preferably with a Teflon-based grease—and reinstalled. Bulkhead-mounted wheels sometimes become stiff due to swelling of a wooden bulkhead around the wheel shaft when the wood gets wet. This can only be cured by enlarging the hole in the bulkhead.

Geared Units

Rack-and-pinion and worm-drive steering units are generally rugged and long lived. In time, some play may develop in rack-and-pinion bushings and gears, which, if left unchecked, may lead to the drive sprocket jumping and tooth damage to both gear and quadrant.

On either side of the drive sprocket, or gear, is a bearing consisting of a bushing and bearing cap. The bushings may be in one piece or two halves. Worn bushings can be temporarily

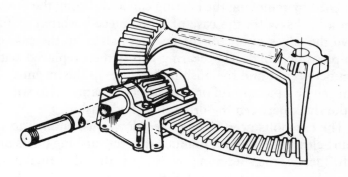

Above and below: *Rack-and-pinion steering.*

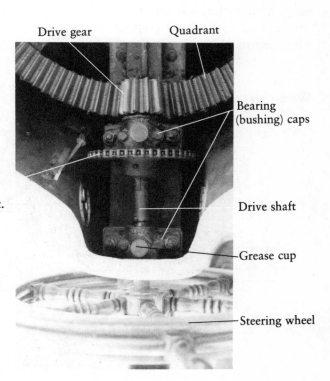

tightened by removing the bearing cap and slitting the bushing with a hacksaw (in the case of a one-piece bushing) or filing down the edges of one of the bearing halves (in the case of a two-piece bushing). The bearing cap is then replaced with a shim between it and the bushing to close up the bushing. The shim can be a piece of tin or even layers of paper. This will take up the slack between the drive shaft and bushing.

The cap bolts need to be pulled down just enough to take up any clearance, but not so much that the bushing binds on its shaft. Ideally, the shimming will be just the right thickness to allow the cap bolts to be tightly fastened. The whole unit should be rebuilt at the earliest opportunity.

Another way of closing up a worn gear and quadrant is to fix a shim on the base plate of the gear unit under the quadrant (if there is a base plate) to hold the quadrant in contact with the gear. Otherwise, loosen the quadrant on the rudder shaft, move it up into closer contact with its drive gear, and then retighten its clamp bolts.

Worm steerer.

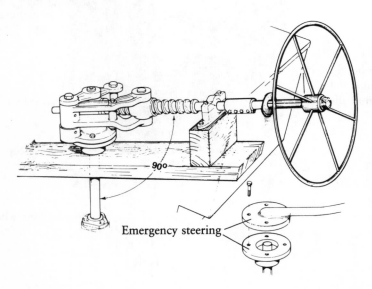

Emergency steering

RACK-AND-PINION WHEEL STEERING FAILURES: QUICK REFERENCE

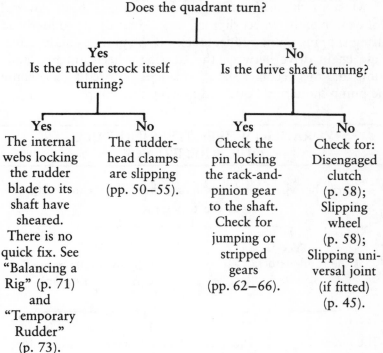

Turn the wheel while observing the rudderhead quadrant. Does the quadrant turn?

Yes
Is the rudder stock itself turning?

No
Is the drive shaft turning?

Yes
The internal webs locking the rudder blade to its shaft have sheared. There is no quick fix. See "Balancing a Rig" (p. 71) and "Temporary Rudder" (p. 73).

No
The rudder-head clamps are slipping (pp. 50–55).

Yes
Check the pin locking the rack-and-pinion gear to the shaft. Check for jumping or stripped gears (pp. 62–66).

No
Check for: Disengaged clutch (p. 58); Slipping wheel (p. 58); Slipping universal joint (if fitted) (p. 45).

In time, worm-drive units develop play in the various linkages and between the worm gears and *traversing nuts* (the nuts that travel up and down the gears to operate the unit). The rudder will start to rock backward and forward ceaselessly, especially at anchor, accelerating the rate of wear. It is time to renew the clevis and hinge pins, and perhaps drill out and bush the pivot points on the arms. The unit had better have been kept lubricated or it will prove almost impossible to disassemble. Be sure to label all parts for reassembly as they come off. If serious play is developing between the worm gears and traversing nuts, the threads in the nuts (which are made of babbitt, a relatively soft white metal used for bearing surfaces in engines) are renewable. This cannot be done at sea.

Hydraulic Steering

Most mechanical difficulties have already been covered (for example, the wheel slipping on its shaft or the rudderhead fitting slipping on its rudder stock). If the unit has an intermediate chain drive between the steering wheel and hydraulic pump and this becomes slack, tension is restored by loosening the pump mounting bolts and moving the pump.

HYDRAULIC WHEEL STEERING FAILURES: QUICK REFERENCE

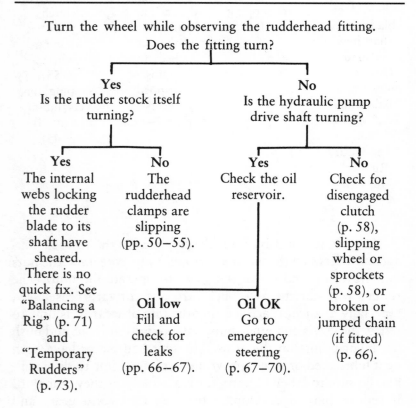

Turn the wheel while observing the rudderhead fitting. Does the fitting turn?

Yes
Is the rudder stock itself turning?

No
Is the hydraulic pump drive shaft turning?

Yes
The internal webs locking the rudder blade to its shaft have sheared. There is no quick fix. See "Balancing a Rig" (p. 71) and "Temporary Rudders" (p. 73).

No
The rudderhead clamps are slipping (pp. 50–55).

Yes
Check the oil reservoir.

No
Check for disengaged clutch (p. 58), slipping wheel or sprockets (p. 58), or broken or jumped chain (if fitted) (p. 66).

Oil low
Fill and check for leaks (pp. 66–67).

Oil OK
Go to emergency steering (p. 67–70).

The most likely cause of a loss of drive from the hydraulic system is an oil leak. All hose connections and shaft and piston seals should be checked, the hoses inspected for chafe wherever they pass through bulkheads, and the unit topped up with oil. Before removing the fill plug make sure the surrounding area is spotlessly clean—hydraulic systems cannot tolerate any dirt.

Hydraulic pumps and pistons are extremely precise pieces of equipment and it is not advisable to open them up. Replacing shaft and piston seals is tricky at sea, even if spare seals are carried on board. If topping up the oil fails to restore drive, it would be better to revert to emergency steering procedures rather than start tearing things apart.

Emergency Tillers

All wheel-steered systems must have some means of shipping an emergency tiller. A solid rudder stock should project 2 or 3 inches above its quadrant or wheel and be squared off to take a tiller. Hollow stocks can be adapted by inserting a pin through the stock and then sliding the slotted emergency tiller

Emergency tiller arrangements.

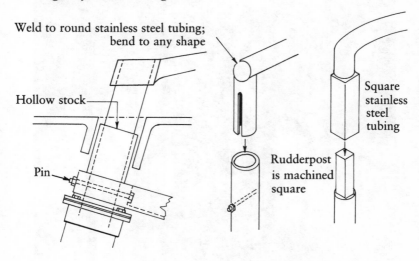

Weld to round stainless steel tubing; bend to any shape

Hollow stock

Pin

Rudderpost is machined square

Square stainless steel tubing

inside the stock and over the pin. Worm-gear units have to be unbolted from their rudderhead flange and a flanged tiller bolted on. If no tiller is available, a pipe (Stillson) wrench or large crescent (adjustable) wrench will provide some leverage and control, which can be amplified via lines taken to cockpit winches, or by block and tackle.

An emergency tiller. Notice how high it must go to clear the binnacle and steering wheel. Because of the tall vertical section, this tiller would be susceptible to bending under load.

It is essential for boat owners with wheel steering to practice fitting an emergency tiller *before* a crisis develops—there may be some surprises. For example, the pedestal on many boats obstructs any emergency tiller. It may be necessary to have one especially constructed to curve up and over the pedestal if you are to obtain any leverage and helming ability. The higher the tiller, however, the less effective and more prone to failure it will be. If there is sufficient room it is preferable to go *around* the binnacle. Also, make sure your boat provides some access to the rudderhead. Without such access, it may prove necessary to cut away the cockpit floor in a crisis.

Any tiller coming over or around a binnacle should be of nonmagnetic material or else it will throw the compass off. It is also one thing to fit such a cumbersome apparatus in a calm anchorage, but quite another to do it in a seaway with the rudder weaving from side to side. It is far easier to fit a short "stub" tiller (say 18 inches long) to bring the rudder under control, and then to slip the main part of the tiller over this stub (or clamp onto it) for proper helming ability.

If an emergency tiller cannot be fitted, another means of rudder control must be found. Some rudders have a hole in their top rear edge, and if lines can be fastened to the back of the rudder and then brought back on board via blocks on each

Recommended emergency tiller configuration to gain sufficient leverage when a binnacle interferes.

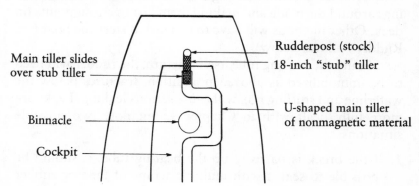

Main tiller slides over stub tiller

Binnacle

Cockpit

Rudderpost (stock)

18-inch "stub" tiller

U-shaped main tiller of nonmagnetic material

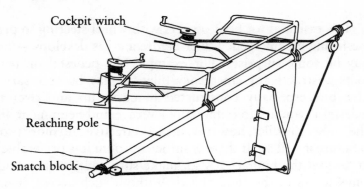

Cockpit winch

Reaching pole

Snatch block

Emergency steering: attaching lines to the rear edge of a rudder.

quarter, you can control the rudder by hand or with the cockpit winches.

Stuffing Box, Bearing, and Bearing Tube Failures

The bearings on shaft-mounted rudders are normally Delrin (or some other kind of plastic) bushings. Should these break, the rudder can start banging around quite violently and do a considerable amount of damage. Immobilize it by placing lashings around the blade and making them fast to strongpoints on deck. Other methods will have to be used to steer the boat (see Rudder Failures below).

Should the bearing tube itself fracture, the rudder will need to be immobilized as above. In addition, fractures below the waterline and stuffing box will cause serious leaking. Leaks are more fully dealt with in Chapter 4, but note two possible situations:

1. If the break is partway up the bearing tube, it should be possible to seal it with multiple wraps of tape or rubber

inner tube reinforced with hose clamps, or by slitting a length of hose and clamping it around the tube.

2. If the bearing tube is fractured where it joins the hull, about the only solution for a quick fix is underwater epoxy. The bearing tube must remain absolutely still while the epoxy cures and must not be subjected to any loads thereafter. Dropping the rudder out of the boat may be necessary to achieve a seal. If so, maneuver a collision mat (see page 101) over the hole to lessen the influx of water.

Stuffing boxes (packing glands) are covered in the next chapter. The principles are exactly the same for a rudder as for a propeller shaft.

Rudder Failures

In one corner of our local boatyard is a pile of broken spade rudders. Almost all are lightweight with hollow stocks. With no protecting keel or skeg, the slightest grounding bends the stock where it enters the lower bearing. Straightening is not advisable; the stresses weaken the rudder at its most loaded point and are likely to lead to later failure. Boat owners with spade rudders would be well advised to learn how to sail without one!

Balancing a Rig

The principles of steering with sails are simple enough. The force of the wind blowing into a main, and especially a mizzen, tends to pivot the boat around the mast and into the wind. The wind blowing against any foresail tends to blow the boat's head off. To hold a course without a rudder these two forces must be in balance. The further a sail is from the turning point of the boat, the greater its leverage. Jibs on long bowsprits and mizzens have a considerable effect—just a few inches of adjustment on the sheets will change the boat's heading.

Bent (left) *and broken spade rudders.*

To counteract a tendency to turn to windward, loosen the sheets of the main and mizzen, moving the booms outboard, or perhaps reef down. An overtrimmed headsail will also help to hold the head off. In extreme cases of weather helm, dragging a drogue from the end of a spinnaker pole or main boom swung out to leeward may counteract it. A bucket or a length of chain might be all that is needed.

To counterbalance a tendency to fall off the wind, the headsail sheet must be slacked, or else a change made to a smaller headsail. Alternatively, a main or mizzen can be sheeted in a little harder.

When running downwind, setting twin jibs on spinnaker or whisker poles and dropping the main and mizzen will probably provide the most control. The course can then be adjusted by tinkering with the sheets.

Next time you take your boat out, let the tiller or wheel go and try balancing the boat and holding a course without it. Try this on different points of sail. It is a rare boat that cannot be controlled with sufficient experimentation.

Temporary Rudders

I have deliberately left the construction of jury-rigged sweeps or rudders until the last. It is next to impossible with the materials available to construct anything that can handle actual steering loads. The best that can be hoped for is to assist an already balanced rig.

Many self-steering systems have an auxiliary rudder that can be pressed into service. Otherwise, the most likely candidate in an emergency is a good solid dinghy oar with a couple of locker covers screwed and lashed to it. If no oar is long or strong enough, a main or mizzen boom would suffice. Many spinnaker and reaching poles will not do; they are designed for compression loading and will collapse under side loads. Whatever is used will, at best, be a temporary expedient in any kind of a seaway—the lashings will work loose and screws pull out.

Jury-rigged rudder.

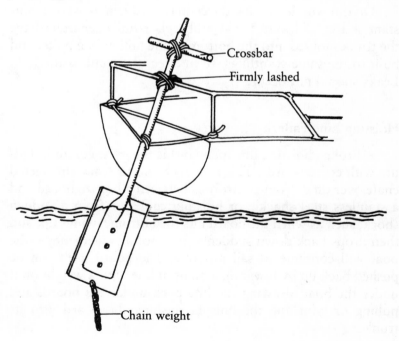

Crossbar

Firmly lashed

Chain weight

The emergency rudder will need some kind of a T bar to the handle so that the blade can be held at the correct angle to the water, it will need a firm lashing to the stern pulpit to provide a pivot point, and its lower end will probably want weighting to keep it in the water.

Centerboards

A centerboard pivots on a hinge pin and is raised by a rope or cable into its trunk, or housing. All very simple, and few problems arise. Some centerboards are designed merely to increase draft and are therefore lightweight. Others incorporate a portion of the boat's ballast (sometimes called a "dropped keel" or "swing keel") and even on a modest-sized sailboat may weigh a ton or more. If problems do occur with ballasted "centerboards" they are rarely easy to solve at sea.

On old wooden boats, the centerboard trunks were a constant source of leaks. Today's fiberglass hulls generally have the trunk molded into the bottom of the hull in one piece, and built to the same scantlings, so in effect the trunk *is* the hull. Leaks should not occur.

Hoisting Line Failure

A broken hoisting line (pendant) is the most common failure with centerboards. This is likely to occur from undetected chafe over time, from electrolysis between a bronze board and a stainless steel shackle or hoisting cable, or from a sudden shock, such as when the board hits the bottom, swings up, and then drops back down suddenly. It is not an emergency—the boat will continue to sail just fine. The board itself can be pushed back up by lowering a bight of line with a weight on it under the boat, drawing the line back under the board, and pulling or winching the line in, pushing the board into its trunk.

Centerboards with hoisting cables attached to the trailing edge generally have a hatch at the top of the trunk providing access to the cable attachment point when the board is up. On other boats, the board is locked to its hinge pin, which projects into the boat. A lever is clamped to the end of the hinge pin, and the hoisting cable is attached to this lever and used to raise or lower the board. With this system the whole cable is accessible from within the boat and easily repaired or replaced. (Note: The hinge pin will be below sea level and a stuffing box (packing gland) is needed to seal it where it enters the boat. Stuffing box leaks are covered in Chapter 4.)

Bent and Jammed Boards

Centerboards should not be raised or lowered when a boat is hard on the wind. The sideways pressure generated by the boat's leeway is liable to jam the board in its trunk and lead to breakage. Similarly, a centerboard bent by running aground hard at an angle will have to be left down until the boat can be hauled and the board pulled out and straightened. Trying to force it into its trunk before this is done will most likely create expensive problems.

Pivot Pin Wear and Failure

In time, wear develops between the hinge pin and its bushings, allowing the board to flex from side to side, probably with an annoying "clunk." When the boat is next hauled the pin and bushings will need to be inspected and renewed as necessary.

In extreme cases, the pivot pin can fail or fall out. The centerboard will then drop out of the boat, probably breaking its hoisting line and going to the bottom. If it does initially hang by its cable, it can do considerable damage as it crashes around, particularly if the board is ballasted. There is no practical way to put a board back at sea. Unless it can be raised on deck or lashed extremely securely to the bottom of the boat, it may be necessary to cut it loose and let it go. Otherwise, it will be quite capable of knocking a hole in the hull.

Sailing without a Centerboard

Without its centerboard, a boat will go downwind just fine; on any kind of a beat, however, the boat will make a tremendous amount of leeway. If the board also incorporated ballast, the boat will be more tender and may be in danger of capsizing, depending on how much ballast is mounted in the keel independently of the centerboard.

Heeling can be lessened by concentrating the sail area as close to the deck as possible. Reef mainsails, and shorten headsails. Tying a figure-eight knot into the top part of a headsail (a "Spanish reef") is one way to reduce heeling potential, but this may damage a wire luff. A headsail luff reinforced with Dacron rope or tape will not be bothered.

Jury-rigged Leeboards

Leeway can be counteracted with improvised leeboards using techniques similar to those for an emergency rudder (fastening bunk boards to an oar, etc.). A leeboard comes under a considerable amount of strain. It should be mounted on the downwind side for maximum immersion, set as deep as possible, and lashed fore and aft as well as to a stanchion. The head of the shaft will also need bracing to a strongpoint on the deck or the base of the mast to keep the leeboard from collapsing under the hull. Motorsailing to maintain a moderate speed will help to counteract the sideways loading.

Since the board will want to twist, a crossbar will be needed to hold it in alignment fore and aft. Using two oars or poles as illustrated, crossed behind the board and both securely lashed on deck, will provide the necessary stiffness.

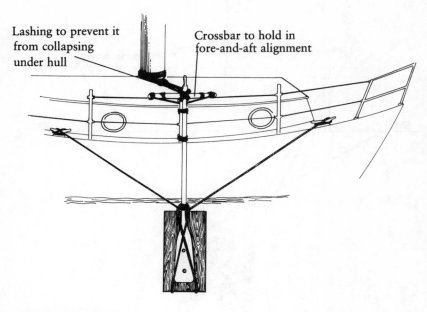

Lashing to prevent it from collapsing under hull

Crossbar to hold in fore-and-aft alignment

Emergency leeboard.

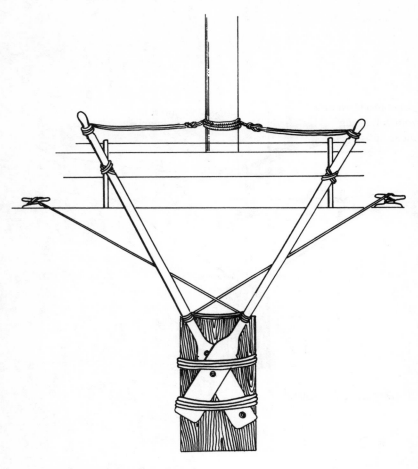

Alternative emergency leeboard.

3

Propellers, Struts, Couplings, and Gearboxes

Propeller Installations

The propeller of an inboard-mounted engine is supported by a bearing at the rear of the boat. In traditional long-keeled boats the propeller shaft exits through the deadwood, and the bearing is inserted in the deadwood itself. On more modern fin-keel

Propeller installation for a long keel and attached rudder.

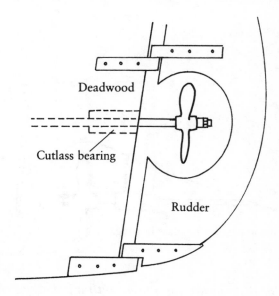

Deadwood

Cutlass bearing

Rudder

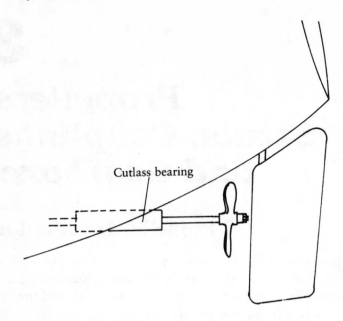

Propeller installation on a boat with a spade rudder.

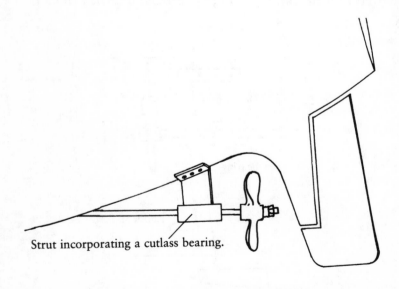

Propeller installation on a boat with a half-skeg rudder.

designs, the bearing is built into the underbody of the hull or placed in a separate strut attached to the hull bottom. The type of bearing used is almost always a "cutlass" bearing—a ribbed rubber sleeve with seawater circulating in it to keep the shaft cool and lubricated.

Fouled Lines

The most common problem with a propeller is fouling one's own lines! Anyone who has done this will know that clearing a fouled propeller can be the devil of a job. Sometimes this can be done by setting the gearbox in neutral and pulling on the rope while rotating the propeller shaft by hand. If this fails, there is generally no choice but to dive down and cut it free. It pays to have a wet suit, snorkel, and fins on board. A knife with a serrated edge will cut through tangled lines better than one with a straight edge; even a hacksaw may prove necessary.

Removing Propellers

Propellers fit on a tapered shaft with a keyway, and are held in place with a nut, locked to the shaft with a cotter pin. There may also be a "fairing" cap screwed onto the back of the propeller hub, over the nut, to reduce water turbulence.

If propeller blades are bent, under no circumstances should any attempt be made to straighten them in place. You could bend the propeller shaft! However, removing a propeller is not easy, especially in the water, and on a number of poorly designed boats it is impossible without first dropping the rudder or pulling the entire engine and propeller shaft forward. (Designers of these boats are good candidates for a firing squad.) Assuming there is enough clearance to pull the propeller off its shaft, normally a special "puller" is used. Without one on board, the problem becomes one of breaking the grip of the tapered shaft on the propeller hub. To make the job easier, the aft end of the boat should be raised as high as possible. This can be done by moving heavy gear forward and perhaps by hanging the dinghy from the bowsprit or stemhead and pumping it full of water.

The propeller nut should be backed out two or three turns, *but not removed until the propeller is loose.* The shaft must be turned so that the keyway is uppermost, since we don't want the key falling out and sinking to the bottom of the ocean. If the propeller will not pull free, it needs to be given a smart blow with a block of wood and a hammer behind its boss, or

Details of a propeller installation.

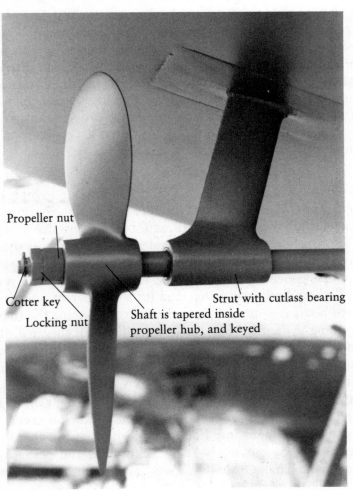

Propeller nut

Cotter key

Locking nut

Shaft is tapered inside propeller hub, and keyed

Strut with cutlass bearing

hub. Try hitting it first behind the keyway (this is the most likely point of binding) and then 180 degrees farther around. If this fails, try heating the hub with a propane torch and then hit it again.

Struts

On so many boats struts are inadequately mounted and under the vibrations from a fouled or bent propeller work loose or crack the surrounding fiberglass. Loose struts allow the propeller and shaft to vibrate and the cutlass bearing to wear, and in time the gearbox oil seal and rear bearing will be ruined.

Unless the boat is hauled, there is little to be done to fix a strut fiberglassed in place. Bolted-on struts are generally fastened with countersunk machine screws, which should be accessible from within the boat. Trying to tighten loose nuts, however, will probably just result in the whole screw turning. The trick is to grip the top of the screw threads with a pair of Vise-Grips or a small pipe wrench and then pull the nuts up tightly. This will do some damage to the screw threads, but that is a small price to pay to save the cutlass or gearbox bearing.

Shaft Couplings

Propeller shafts will sometimes work loose inside their couplings. In extreme cases when the engine is put in reverse, the propeller pulls the shaft out the back of the boat or into the rudder.

In a decent installation, a coupling is *keyed* to its shaft and then locked in place with a pin, through-bolt, or set screws. All too many couplings omit the key and rely just on pins, bolts, or set screws. Should these shear off or slip, however, it is a simple matter to fit another bolt or tighten down the existing screws. Set screws must first be realigned with their "dimples" in the shaft.

Shaft couplings may be keyed and pinned (top) or pinned and then restrained from slipping by set screws seated in dimples in the propeller shaft (bottom).

Gearbox Failures

Most of today's sailboats use hydraulic gearboxes (transmissions) with remote controls. An oil pump generates pressure within the gearbox. Moving the gear lever switches the direction of the oil flow, thus engaging forward or reverse gears. Unlike the old manual boxes, very little external pressure is needed to engage gears.

The control cables are of the push-pull type; moving the gear lever in one direction causes the cable to push on the gearbox operating lever, while movement in the other direction will cause the cable to exert a pull.

The following problems with hydraulic gearboxes are relatively easy to identify and fix:

1. No forward or reverse. Check first to see that the remote control is actually moving the gearbox lever. If it is, check the gearbox oil level and top up as necessary. Low oil will cause air to be sucked into the hydraulic circuit. This is frequently accompanied by a buzzing noise. Adding oil and running the engine in neutral will clear out the air. Be sure to find out how the oil is being lost and have the problem corrected as soon as possible. If the boat still has no forward or reverse see if the gearbox output coupling is turning. If it is, the gearbox is OK, and the coupling has either sheared its bolts or is slipping on its shaft. The shaft will sometimes pull right out of the coupling; the propeller itself may even have come off.

2. Stiff operation of the control lever. Disconnect the cable from the gearbox and try again. If the lever is still stiff the control cable needs to be removed from its conduit, cleaned, greased (preferably with Teflon-based grease), and reinstalled. If the stiffness is in the gearbox, have it looked at as soon as possible.

3. Improper operation of forward or reverse, or stuck in one gear. Problems with the control cable should once again be suspected first. Check not only that the remote control is

GEARBOX (TRANSMISSION) PROBLEMS:
QUICK REFERENCE

Operate the remote control lever. Does it move the gearbox lever?

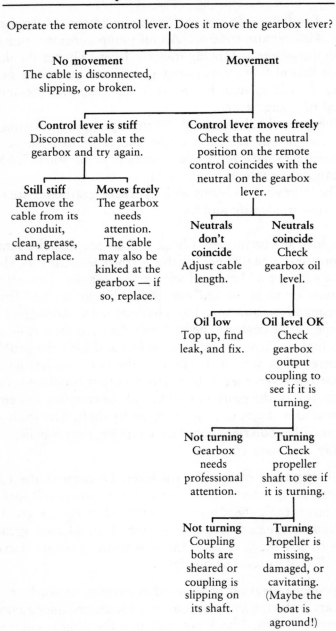

No movement
The cable is disconnected,
slipping, or broken.

Movement

Control lever is stiff
Disconnect cable at the
gearbox and try again.

Control lever moves freely
Check that the neutral
position on the remote
control coincides with the
neutral on the gearbox
lever.

Still stiff
Remove the
cable from its
conduit,
clean, grease,
and replace.

Moves freely
The gearbox
needs
attention.
The cable
may also be
kinked at the
gearbox — if
so, replace.

**Neutrals
don't
coincide**
Adjust cable
length.

**Neutrals
coincide**
Check
gearbox oil
level.

Oil low
Top up, find
leak, and fix.

Oil level OK
Check
gearbox
output
coupling to
see if it is
turning.

Not turning
Gearbox
needs
professional
attention.

Turning
Check
propeller
shaft to see if
it is turning.

Not turning
Coupling
bolts are
sheared or
coupling is
slipping on
its shaft.

Turning
Propeller is
missing,
damaged, or
cavitating.
(Maybe the
boat is
aground!)

actually moving the gearbox lever, but also that the gearbox lever is in the neutral position when the control is in neutral. If not, adjust the control cable length as necessary. Finally, when the control cable is in the "push" position see that it is not kinking at the gearbox lever, thus restricting the travel of the lever.

4

Leaks

Finding Leaks

When a sailboat first starts taking on water, the level rises at an alarming rate because the bilges, especially on most modern boats, contain very little volume. In no time at all the water is creeping up the settee berths. If this happens at night and in any kind of unpleasant conditions it will be a terrifying experience.

Unless the source of a leak is obvious the first thing to do is *taste* the water. If it is fresh we have nothing more than a holed water tank. Assuming salt water, the most likely sources for the leak are well down in the boat, and any such source is among the first things to go under. Speed in checking all through hulls and hoses is essential. They must be kept accessible and not buried under a mountain of stores. A couple of dummy runs *before* a crisis develops will allow you to see just how fast you can get to all your through hulls, the stuffing box, cockpit drains, and engine cooling hoses. Don't forget the rudder stuffing box if one is fitted.

All seacocks must be closed (except possibly the raw-water supply to the engine if this must be run) and the stuffing box checked. *If this stems the flow of water into the boat a broken hose or some siphonic action is almost certainly the source of the leak* (see below).

If the leak continues, there may be various through hulls (holding tank vents; refrigeration condenser overboard discharge; the engine exhaust pipe) installed above the waterline

---

LEAK DETECTION: QUICK REFERENCE

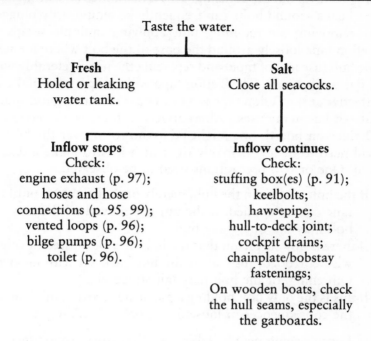

Taste the water.

Fresh	**Salt**
Holed or leaking water tank.	Close all seacocks.

Inflow stops	**Inflow continues**
Check:	Check:
engine exhaust (p. 97);	stuffing box(es) (p. 91);
hoses and hose	keelbolts;
connections (p. 95, 99);	hawsepipe;
vented loops (p. 96);	hull-to-deck joint;
bilge pumps (p. 96);	cockpit drains;
toilet (p. 96).	chainplate/bobstay
	fastenings;
	On wooden boats, check
	the hull seams, especially
	the garboards.

---

without seacocks. *Suspect every one,* especially if the boat is heeled. Simply coming about onto the other tack may stop the leak. An unplugged hawsepipe down to a chain locker can let in large amounts of water when punching into head seas. Similarly, broken deck or cockpit scuppers will funnel a lot of water aboard, and with the rail under, considerable amounts of water may find a way below past poor hull-to-deck joints. If the engine is running and the exhaust is holed, the raw-water pump will steadily empty water into the boat.

All through-bolted fixtures in the hull need checking. Loose rigging is often a clue to failed chainplate or bobstay attachments. A friend had his 53-foot Alden schooner go to the bottom when electrolysis ate away the mounting bolts to his bobstay fitting, which was just below the waterline. If a fastening is suspect but is hidden behind interior joinery, for good-ness' sake rip out the paneling. This is no time to be sentimental!

Leaks around bolts can frequently be temporarily plugged by removing the retaining nut, applying multiple wraps of Teflon tape loosely around the base of the bolt where it enters the hull (use lots of tape) and replacing the nut, preferably with a flat washer first. The Teflon tape will compress to make an effective seal. (Teflon tape is an essential item in a good spares kit—it has many uses.) Alternatively, if there is a selection of O-rings on board, one might be found to fit over the bolt. It will need to be a reasonably tight fit if it is to make a decent seal. One or two precautions need to be observed:

• If the bolt is loose in the hull, merely back the nut off until the tape can be applied. If the nut is removed all the way the bolt may fall out of the hull.
• If there is any suspicion that the bolt may be wasted or other-wise corroded, just pinch the nut back up without over-tightening, or the bolt may fail altogether.
• If this is the only bolt holding a particular fixture, think about the consequences of loosening it before undoing it.

Loose rigging may be telling another story. Sometimes the compression loads on a mast will drive it through the bottom of a boat. On wooden boats, the garboard (bottom plank) seams will open up. On fiberglass boats, in extreme cases, the laminate will crack. One well-known boatbuilder recently had a team touring the country rebuilding and reinforcing the keel mast step on a new model after several owners had collapsed their steps onto the keels of their boats by cranking down on the backstay adjuster!

Wooden or fiberglass boats with external ballast are prone to leaking around the keelbolts. Wasted bolts may fail without warning, letting in large amounts of water. This kind of leak is hard to find as it will quickly be covered by the inflow, and the bolts are often hidden beneath tanks or other equipment. The boat may have to be pumped completely dry before the inflow can be spotted. Nine times out of ten the most expedient and perhaps the only solution is to keep pumping until you can haul the boat and have all keelbolts checked and replaced as necessary. Meantime, you should treat the boat gently to keep as much stress as possible off the keel.

—— Stuffing Boxes (Packing Glands)

Where the propeller shaft on an inboard engine enters the boat, a seal known as *a stuffing box* or *packing gland* keeps the water out. Some stuffing boxes are rigidly mounted and incorporate a shaft bearing. Others are attached to the bearing with a length of hose and are known as flexible stuffing boxes.

A stuffing box consists of a threaded tube that fits over the propeller shaft, the space between the shaft and tube being filled with "packing." A nut is screwed down onto the packing, compressing it until it forms a seal around the shaft. The same arrangement seals many rudder stocks.

Packing almost always consists of a special type of graphite- or grease-impregnated square-sided fiber (flax) rope, although sometimes a form of graphite tape is used. The rope is cut into rings using a diagonal cut so that the ends overlap when in place. Three or four rings are slid around the shaft and up into the box with their joints widely staggered. A compression sleeve or liner is placed on top, and the packing nut is attached.

Adjusting Packing

The idea is not to stop all water coming into the boat, but to slow it to a drip. Overtightening packing nuts is a common error. The packing then binds on the shaft and the friction wears grooves in the shaft, which becomes almost impossible to seal. A packing nut should be tightened just a little at a time while rotating the shaft by hand. When the packing begins to bind on the shaft, back out the nut an eighth of a turn. Now start the engine and engage the propeller. After the shaft has been spinning for a minute or two, shut down the motor and

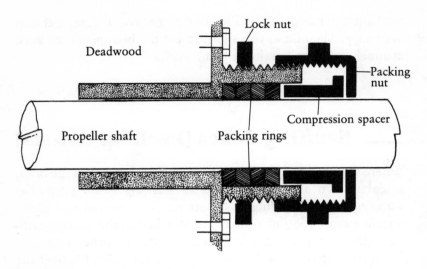

Cross section of a rigid stuffing box.

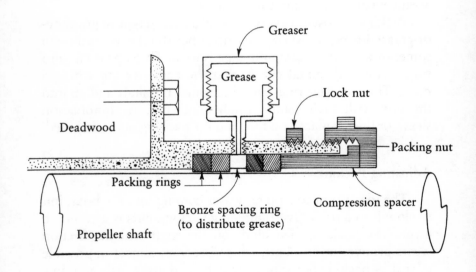

Cross section of a stuffing box with grease fitting. The greaser with a screwdown cap may be replaced with a grease nipple or remote greaser.

feel the shaft where it emerges from the stuffing box. If it is warm, the packing is too tight. If the shaft cannot be sealed without overtightening the nut, the packing needs to be replaced.

Replacing the Packing

Digging out old packing requires a special tool—a corkscrew mounted on a flexible handle, available from tool supply outfits. Unfortunately, few sailors seem to carry one, or spare packing. It is almost impossible to dig all the old packing from many stuffing boxes without this tool, and attempts to do so using knives, ice picks, and so on almost invariably leave odd pieces behind. Any new packing then fails to seat properly, frequently making matters worse rather than better. If this tool is not available it is best to leave things alone. Faced with severe leaks that cannot be cured by tightening the packing nut,

Rigid stuffing boxes (top) *and a flexible stuffing box* (bottom). (Courtesy Wilcox Crittenden)

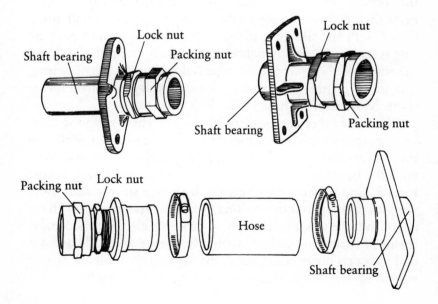

pumping in a load of grease through the grease fitting is a temporary expedient.

If the grease fails to stem the leak, or if your stuffing box has no grease fitting, 1/4-inch manila rope (or strands off a larger rope) cut to size, heavily impregnated with grease, and slid up in the stuffing box on top of the existing packing will have some effect. *Do not use synthetic rope.* It is too hard and may damage the shaft, if it doesn't melt.

If you are properly equipped and decide to replace the packing, remember that *all* the old packing must first be removed. Sometimes a bronze spacing (lubricating) ring is fitted between packing rings—if so, note its position and put it back in the same place. Packing comes in precut rings (by far the best) or in rolls, in which case the rings must be cut to fit (the packing is wrapped around the shaft three or four times and a diagonal cut made across the wraps with a *very sharp* knife). The correct size of packing is important; 1/4″, 3/8″, and 1/2″ are common sizes, the size being governed by the space between the shaft and the stuffing box wall.

Each packing ring must be tamped down before the next is installed; otherwise, when the last is in and the packing nut is tightened it will overcompress the last rings and undercompress the first ones. I keep some pieces of pipe slit in half along their length and slip these in the stuffing box after each packing ring is inserted. I *lightly* tighten the packing nut to tamp down the ring and then remove the pipe halves and fit the next ring. The joints on the rings must be widely staggered around the shaft. Most stuffing boxes take four rings.

All this bother can be dispensed with. There is on the market a graphite tape that is merely wrapped around a shaft and then compressed into the stuffing box (full instructions come with the box). It works wonderfully and seems to last almost forever, and when it does begin to leak, one simply adds more without cleaning out the stuffing box. It is expensive, and I have heard that the graphite is likely to promote electrolysis. Nevertheless, I repacked our boat with it five years ago and have not had to touch the packing since, through 1,000 hours of engine running time. So far I have seen no signs of electrolysis.

Failure of the Hose on a Flexible Stuffing Box

A major emergency is possible with a flexible stuffing box if the hose holding it in place comes loose or splits. In either case, water will flood into the boat at an alarming rate.

Merely pushing a loose hose back onto its fitting and reclamping will solve the crisis, but a split hose is not so easy to fix—a new one cannot be put in place without first removing the propeller shaft. The leak can be brought under control with multiple wraps of duct or electrician's tape or by slitting another length of hose, wrapping it around the split, and clamping with hose clamps (or binding tightly in place). The same technique can be used on any other split hoses (cockpit drains, water cooling hoses, etc.). We carry an old inner tube on board—the kind with smooth, not ribbed, rubber. A long strip

A corroded galvanized exhaust elbow. The hot gases and water from the engine exhaust have eaten right through it.

The same corroded exhaust elbow patched with rubber inner tube and hose clamps. This repair held for 200 hours of engine running time!

wrapped a number of times tightly around a damaged hose and clamped in place will make a very effective temporary repair.

_____ **Siphons**

A leaking stuffing box is the most common cause of water entering a boat. A steady trickle unchecked can sink a boat on its moorings in just a few days. But what if we are at sea and all of a sudden there is water bubbling up from the bilges and over the cabin sole. We have hit nothing and a quick check of the stuffing box, through hulls, and all hoses reveals no leaks. Where on earth can it be coming from?

Vented Loops

All bilge pumps, and most toilets and engines, are installed below the waterline. Any time the discharge outlet from a pump, toilet, or raw-water cooling circuit is below water there is potential for siphoning seawater back *into* the boat. To combat this, the discharge lines are generally carried up under the deck, with a "vented loop" installed at the high point.

A vented loop is a very simple device with either a rubber flap or small hole in its top that allows air into a line, breaking any tendency to form a siphon. However, vented loops in salt water are notoriously prone to plug up, or in the case of engine cooling systems, spray a fine mist of salt water all over the engine and its electronics. Sometimes a loop will do both.

A 1½-inch pump or toilet discharge siphoning into a boat can set up a pretty good flow. Normally, some form of a check valve will be in the line, but this is probably no more than a simple rubber flap. In time, the rubber hardens, or swells and fails to seat, or else a matchstick or small piece of paper gets lodged under the flap, and water flows steadily through.

One of the most common causes of siphoning action is the salt water supply to the head (toilet). The toilet rim is almost always below sea level, and if the vented loop on the supply line fails, the toilet will fill and steadily flow into the boat. This has sunk many a boat.

Engine Exhausts

Water also can siphon back into the engine's exhaust pipe, through an open exhaust valve, and into the engine itself. This is most likely to occur when large following seas drive up the

A vented loop on an engine cooling circuit. The hose (top) discharges into the cockpit so that if the vent fails in the open position it will not spray cooling water all over the engine.

back of the boat. If on cranking an engine locks up solidly when previously it has been giving no other signs of trouble, this must be one of the primary suspects. Under no circumstances should it be started; serious damage is likely to occur to the pistons and connecting rods. The engine will need to be turned over a little at a time (with the throttle closed) to ease the water out from the cylinders. When the water is forced out, the starting motor should crank freely. If the engine has decompression levers and a hand start, it should be turned over man-

A toilet siphoning into a boat.

ually until it turns easily. If the water finds its way into the crankcase, the oil will need changing. Only then should the engine be started and idled for a while to drive the remaining water out.

Remedies

If closing all seacocks stems the flow of water into a boat, a broken hose or some siphoning action is almost certainly the culprit. With a little luck, a few strokes on the toilet and bilge pumps will clear the valves and seat them correctly. A vented loop is easily fixed by unscrewing its cap and washing it in fresh warm water to clean out salt crystals and anything else plugging it up. In the case of engine cooling circuits it is advisable to put a piece of tubing over the cap and lead this out into the cockpit or down into the bilges. Then if the loop does begin to spray salt water, it will not damage the engine's electrical circuits.

—————— Through Hulls and Hoses

Even good hoses do not last forever, especially those subjected to heat in the engine cooling system. Any hose that is particularly soft (and perhaps bulging) or hard and cracked *needs replacing right away.*

Hose clamps are a frequent source of trouble. Many stainless steel clamps have nickel-plated steel screws that rapidly rust out in a salt atmosphere. Clamps should be checked (with a magnet) for *all*-stainless construction, which is nonmagnetic. Keep some spares on board and a screwdriver to tighten them.

Failed hoses and through hulls sink many boats. Every through hull should have a tapered softwood plug (a "fid") tied to it so that in the event of failure the hose can be cut away and the plug hammered up the through hull to seal it. However, a number of through-hull failures are the result of electrolysis destroying the external fitting, permitting the *entire through hull* to fall out of the hull. Keep some fids on board large enough to plug a hole this size.

Major Leaks

Immediate Action

Faced with a rapid influx of water, pumping will be of only limited use. Any serious leaks will overwhelm the pumps found on the majority of boats. If the boat is not to founder *the leak must be stemmed as a first priority.* It is necessary to be quite ruthless, ripping out interior joinery and cabinetwork as necessary.

"Proper" seacock installation. A tapered softwood plug (not shown) should be attached to the fitting with a lanyard.

Two stainless steel hose clamps

A "tail pipe" fitting for the hose

Through bolted

A generous backing block well bedded in caulking compound

MAJOR LEAKS: QUICK REFERENCE

---

1. Find the leak.
2. Bring it as close to the waterline as possible to reduce water pressure (p. 101).
3. Bung it from the inside with boat cushions, etc., to slow the inflow (p. 102).
4. Maneuver a temporary patch over the leak (p. 101).
5. Get on top of the pumping situation (p. 102).
6. Make more permanent repairs (p. 106).

Once the leak is found, bring it as close to the waterline as possible. Water pressure, and therefore the rate of inflow, increases rapidly with depth. (Conversely, as the waterline *inside* the boat approaches that outside, the rate of influx slows.) If necessary, put the boat on a broad reach, sheet the sails in hard, and put the beam ends of the opposite side of the boat in the water. (Don't do this if it becomes impossible to work on the leak or if the boat speed is driving water through the hole. Use your common sense.)

Remember, if shorthanded and faced with a choice between plugging and pumping, *plug first*!

Immediate Repairs

In theory, the best way to fix a serious leak is to deploy a collision mat over the source. A collision mat is a circular piece of canvas with five or six grommets sewn into its perimeter. Lines are spliced into the grommets. After the mat is pulled down under the hull and drawn up tightly, water pressure is supposed to hold it in place over the hole.

Yet I know of no boat that carries a collision mat. However, one could use any small, heavyweight sail (for example, a storm trysail or jib) with lines attached to the three corners.

One or more corners will need to be weighted to pull the sail down so that it can be dragged under the boat. As anyone who has dropped a headsail in the water and had it dragged under the boat will know, it is hard to maneuver pieces of fabric in these circumstances, especially if the bottom is at all foul with barnacles. Besides, collision mats might work well on rounded boat bottoms, but not with keels, skegs, struts, rudders, and other obstructions.

The best bet for immediate damage control with serious leaks is often to bung up the hole from inside the boat with cushions, towels, or whatever is handy and to shore this in place. If necessary, rip out interior joinery to gain access. Once everything is under control, it may be possible to maneuver an external patch over the hole. Having a wetsuit, mask, snorkel and fins on board will greatly ease inspection and underwater work.

One other device available from some marine stores is a collision "umbrella." This is, quite literally, a small umbrella that is poked through any hole *from the inside* and then opened out. Water pressure then is supposed to hold it against the hull side. I have never used one, nor heard of one being used, but it sounds like a good idea.

Pumping and Bailing

Failure of the pumps is a common cause of unnecessary founderings. Emergencies most commonly arise in rough seas with the water sloshing around in the cabin, and this washes all kinds of debris into the bilges (matchsticks and cigarette wrappers being two of the most troublesome) while admitting slugs of air into any pumps.

The old piston and rotary pumps are not self-priming and cannot tolerate any trash. They have no place as bilge pumps on boats, and are fortunately not often seen any longer. It is quite remarkable, however, how many people depend entirely on electric centrifugal bilge pumps. These are great for everyday use, but what happens when the water comes up over the batteries and shorts them out? Since batteries are generally well down in the bilges, they are often among the first things to go. (On our boat we have accepted the weight penalty and mounted them under the deckhead; all wiring is also as high as possible in the boat.) There is just no substitute for a large-capacity manual diaphragm pump—these are self-priming and can tolerate surprisingly large particles. Every boat should have at least one.

Diaphragm Pumps. There is almost nothing to go wrong in a diaphragm pump. If the pump handle cannot be stroked backward and forward, the discharge seacock is probably closed. If the handle is moving but the pump fails to operate, the first thing to check is the "strum box"—the filter on the end of the intake hose. It will quite likely be plugged, perhaps with the label off some canned goods or a plastic bag. Another possibility is a collapsed hose, normally on the intake side.

If either flap fails to seat, the pump will not work. Common causes of flap failure are trash on the seat; swelled rubber from chemicals in the bilges, especially oil and diesel; and hard rubber from old age, heat, or chemicals.

The innards of some pumps (for example, Whale) are immediately accessible by undoing a handwheel and hinging open the whole side of the pump. On others (for example, Edson, Henderson, ITT) the inlet and outlet valve assemblies can be unbolted from the pump body. In either case, if the pump is below sea level the discharge seacock must first be closed.

The valve seats will need cleaning. A swelled rubber flap can be made temporarily serviceable by trimming its perimeter with a knife until it will move up and down without hanging up on its housing. However, a pump overhaul kit (see the Appendix) is one of those essential items that should be kept on board at all times so that new valves can be substituted.

Diaphragms eventually fail. Once again, replacement is simply a matter of unbolting the relevant housing and then undoing a central bolt that passes through a plate on either side of the diaphragm and into the pump handle socket. *What is absolutely essential when replacing valves and diaphragms is to make sure that all the seating surfaces in the pump are thoroughly cleaned before reassembly.* Otherwise the pump will leak and probably not work.

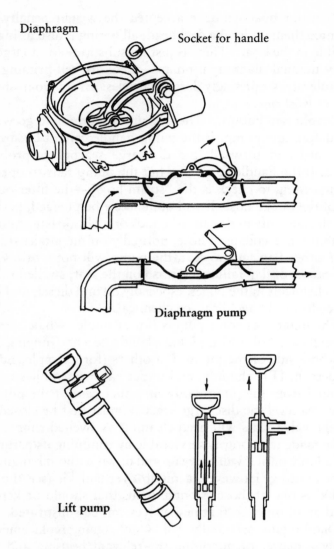

Diaphragm

Socket for handle

Diaphragm pump

Lift pump

The pumping action of a diaphragm pump and a lift pump.
(Drawings by Jim Sollers)

Finally, diaphragm pump handles have a tendency to fatigue and fail where they fit onto the pump. Carry a spare handle.

Engine-Driven Pumps. A big enough leak will soon overwhelm any manual pump, while an auxiliary engine–driven pump will move a lot of water and free up the crew for leak detection and repair. These pumps are not particularly expensive and are a highly recommended piece of add-on equipment.

A vertically mounted diaphragm pump (shown here with the retaining ring removed), such as one mounted on the side of a cockpit well, makes for a very comfortable pumping position, but the combination of a leaking diaphragm (salt water), a stainless steel hinge pin, and an aluminum pump body ensures that it will not be long before this handle is frozen up.

The two best options are centrifugal and rubber-impeller pumps. Centrifugal pumps are not self-priming, so to be of any use in an emergency they must be set low enough in the boat and the intake so designed that they will fill with water if a serious leak develops. Their impellers, being metal, are almost indestructible, and these pumps can run dry almost indefinitely.

Rubber-impeller pumps (for example, the Jabsco pumps) are self-priming, but their impellers cannot tolerate being run dry for more than a few seconds. It is essential to carry a good supply of spare impellers and to install the pump so that it is readily accessible for impeller replacement.

All engine-driven pumps are likely to suffer from slipping belts once the water in the boat is up to the pulleys. To lessen this the belts must be kept properly tensioned at all times.

Diesel engines will continue to run until the air intake goes under water or until water can find its way into the crankcase (for example, via the dipstick hole). If the raw-water supply is removed from its seacock (be sure to close the seacock first!), pushed down in the bilges, and the engine cranked, the motor will pump water from the bilges out of the exhaust. Similarly, the suction from any other pumps (such as a refrigeration condenser cooling pump or an engine-driven saltwater washdown pump) can be placed in the bilges. Some kind of a strainer must be improvised to protect these pumps and the engine. This need be no more than a can punched full of holes.

Bailing.   Once the water level is well up in the cabin the most effective means of removing it will be to bail with a bucket, throwing the water out the companionway hatch. With sufficient adrenalin one can work a bucket for unbelievable periods of time.

More Permanent Repairs

So far as possible, make repairs *from the outside* —water pressure will help to hold patches in place. Bunk boards and pieces of paneling or bulkheads can be nailed up on wooden boats, but on fiberglass, steel, and aluminum, some form of bracing is needed across the hole on the inside. Screws can then be put through the brace into the patch on the outside. The patch will need sufficient body to hold the fastenings. The advantage of this method is that the fastening is done from within the boat.

Laying the patch over an existing collision mat, layers of sailcloth, or even layers of paper will help to seal the edges. Closed cell foam from cockpit cushions or life vests is also excellent.

The best substance for sealing leaks is underwater epoxy. It comes as a paste in two cans. The cans are mixed thoroughly and the putty daubed on by hand. It sticks to wet surfaces and sets underwater in about half an hour, depending on water temperature. Every cruising boat should have some on board —a gallon would not be too much. Polysulfide rubber and silicone sealants will not work underwater because they do not adhere to wet surfaces.

An emergency patch. Seal with underwater epoxy forced in around the edges.

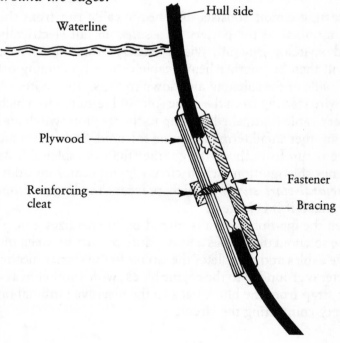

5

Troubleshooting Diesel Engines

Failure to Crank

If an engine refuses to turn over at all, the problem lies in the starting circuit. It may be simply a dead battery, faulty wiring, or a defective switch, solenoid, or starter motor.

Starting Circuits—General Description

A starting circuit consists of a heavy cable run from the positive terminal of the battery to a *solenoid* (an electrically operated switch), generally via a battery isolation switch. There will then be another heavy cable or a strap coming off the other side of the solenoid and down to the starter motor. A smaller wire starting from the same solenoid terminal to which the battery cable is attached runs up to the ignition switch and back to another small terminal on the solenoid. Sometimes the first wire is run from the battery rather than the solenoid. At other times this ignition switch circuit incorporates an additional *neutral start switch,* which prevents the engine from being cranked if it is in gear.

When the ignition switch is turned on, it energizes a magnet in the solenoid that closes a heavy-duty contact between the two large cables and completes the circuit to the starter motor. The starter is grounded to the engine block, with another heavy cable or strap from the block back to the negative terminal on the battery completing the circuit.

FAILURE TO CRANK: QUICK REFERENCE

---

1. **Preliminary Checks**
   LISTEN to the solenoid (p. 109).
   • Rapid clicking = dead battery
   • One loud click = shorted or jammed starter
   • No clicks = defective starting circuit or solenoid
   • "Whirring" = jammed pinion on inertia starter
   FEEL the battery cables — if warm, clean all terminals.
2. **Test procedure** (Note: the battery must be fully charged)
   1. Use a wire to jump the starter switch (p. 110).
   2. Use a screwdriver to jump the solenoid (p. 111).
   3. Check the starter motor (p. 112).

There are two kinds of starter motors: inertia and preengaged. The two are easily distinguished. An inertia starter invariably has an independently mounted solenoid, while a preengaged starter must have its solenoid bolted to the top of it. Inertia motors are found on older engines and outboards with electric starting.

Troubleshooting Starting Circuits

Hot Cables.   At various times, throughout the following test procedures, the battery cables and terminals should be felt to see if they are warm. If they are, disconnect them, thoroughly clean the terminals and cable ends, and then firmly reconnect them. This includes the ground cable as well—its attachment point to the engine block is a frequent source of trouble.

Unusual Noises.   Noise and the voltmeter (which should be installed in the engine instrument panel) can provide essential clues to starting difficulties. A rapid clicking from the solenoid, with the voltage falling off to nothing, almost certainly indicates a dead battery. One loud click followed by the voltage falling off is likely to be the result of a jammed or shorted starter motor. A loud "whirring" from an inertia starter tells us that the motor is spinning but the pinion (drive gear) is not engaging the engine flywheel. No clicks at all is evidence of a defective switch circuit.

Testing an Ignition Switch. To check the ignition switch circuit, connect a wire from the main battery terminal of the solenoid to the small return terminal from the switch, thus bypassing the switch. You may generate a spark, so before this or any of the following tests is carried out all necessary precautions must be taken to vent the engine room of hazardous fumes, *especially on gasoline engines.* If the motor cranks with the switch bypassed, the ignition switch (or the neutral start switch if one is fitted) or its wiring is bad. If nothing happens, the solenoid itself is suspect.

Starting circuit with an inertia starter. To bypass the switch, connect a jumper from A to B. To bypass the switch and solenoid, connect a heavy-duty jumper (for example, a screwdriver) from A to C. (Courtesy OMC)

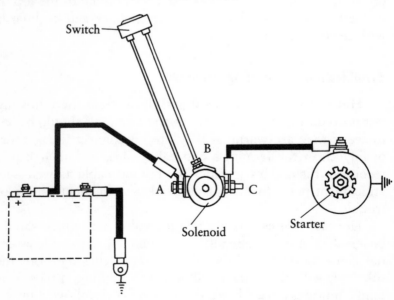

Testing a Solenoid. A solenoid can be jumped (bypassed) by holding a screwdriver blade firmly across its two main heavy-duty terminals. The full starting current of the battery will be flowing through the screwdriver blade, and considerable arcing will occur if it does not make a good contact or if it is allowed to ground out on the starter or solenoid housing. More than enough heat can be generated to melt a big chunk out of the screwdriver! If the starter now spins, the solenoid is defective. If it does not spin, the starter itself is suspect.

Jumping a defective solenoid will crank an engine with an inertia starter. On a preengaged starter, the starter motor will spin but the engine itself cannot be turned over until the solenoid is replaced or repaired.

Starting circuit with a preengaged starter. To bypass the switch, connect a jumper from terminal B to terminal S on the solenoid. To bypass the solenoid and switch, connect a heavy-duty jumper (for example, a screwdriver) from terminal B to terminal M. (Courtesy PCM Marine)

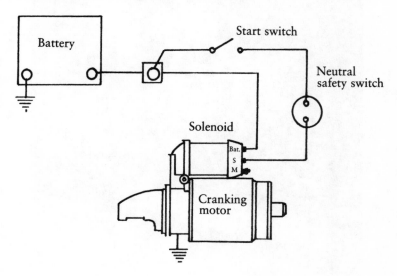

Starter Motor Problems.   Should the tests indicate a problem with the starter, an inertia starter is easier to fix than a preengaged. In the center of the rear housing is a small cover, the removal of which will expose the squared-off end of the drive shaft. A jammed starter can often be freed by placing the appropriate wrench on the shaft and turning it in both directions.

A preengaged starter motor. Jump out the ignition switch by connecting a wire across terminals 1 and 2. Jump out the solenoid with a screwdriver across 1 and 3.

If an inertia starter is "whirring" but not turning the engine over, giving the motor a good smart blow while it is spinning can often make it work. If this fails, unbolt the motor from the engine. The drive pinion is mounted on a shaft with helical grooves cut in it. Clean the grooves so the pinion moves freely up and down the shaft. The starter can then be replaced.

Failure to Start

In essence, a diesel engine is a very simple piece of machinery based on the fact that air heats up as it is compressed. A diesel engine cylinder compresses air until it reaches a temperature of 1,000° F (538° C) or more. Since diesel fuel burns at any temperature above 750° F (399° C), any diesel sprayed ("injected") into this cylinder will catch fire. The fuel injection system on a diesel engine meters out a precise quantity of fuel and injects it into the cylinders at the correct stage of compression, causing the engine to run.

If a diesel has clean air, ignition temperatures, and a correctly timed and atomized injection of fuel, *it has to run.* If the starter motor and switches are okay and the engine is cranking but still won't start, we must methodically check these three things.

Air Supply

A plugged-up air supply is the least likely cause of starting problems, but it only takes a couple of minutes to check the air intake for obstructions and to look at the air filter.

Ignition Temperatures

There are three principal causes for a failure to reach ignition temperatures on initial start-up: Cold weather, slow cranking speeds, and poor compression. They are interrelated, but for clarity, let's treat them separately.

Cold Weather. The colder the incoming air, the more it must be compressed to achieve starting temperatures. The colder the engine surfaces, the more heat of compression is lost to the engine. The colder the engine, the thicker the oil and the more resistance there is to cranking. The colder the battery, the less its output and the slower the engine will turn over.

Slow Cranking Speeds. The slower an engine cranks, the more time there is for the heat of compression to be dissipated to cold engine surfaces, and for the compressed air to escape past poorly sealed valves and piston rings.

Poor Compression. Leaking valves and pistons allow some of the air charge to escape from the cylinder, lowering the

The four cycles of a diesel engine. (1) Inlet stroke. Air is drawn into the cyclinder. (2) Compression. The air is compressed and becomes hot. (3) Injection. Fuel is sprayed into the hot air, ignites, and burns. The high pressure forces down the piston. (4) Exhaust. The burnt gases are evacuated. (Courtesy Lucas CAV)

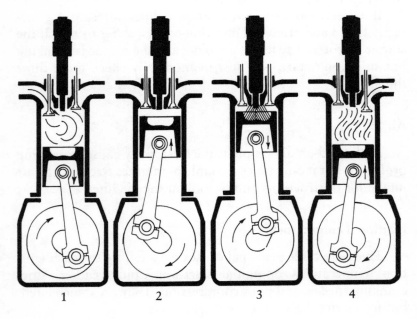

| 1 | 2 | 3 | 4 |

final compression pressure and temperature. Worn bearings increase the size of the compression chamber, lowering overall pressures.

Remedies.   A number of techniques can be used to help an engine reach ignition temperature:

Heat Sources. Most engines have some form of cold-start device for cold weather. The most common are glow plugs, but others include excess fuel injection, heaters or "flame primers" in air inlets, and various oil and ether injection devices. In the event that the cold-start mechanism is insufficient or out of order, any external heat source can be used in difficult starting.

Warming the engine compartment with a kerosene lantern or light bulb may be all that is needed. Gently playing the flame from a propane torch over the inlet manifold and fuel lines will have a marked effect. The flame can also be held *across* the air inlet when the engine is cranked to heat the incoming air. The flame should never be concentrated at any one point on the engine because localized heating may crack engine castings. Nor should the torch be played over wiring harnesses, plastic fittings, or anything combustible. Be sure to vent the engine room thoroughly before you start.

Such methods are used *entirely at the reader's risk.* (I have no control over the dummy who burns through a fuel line and starts a fire!) **Caution:** *These techniques are absolutely out of the question on gasoline engines, or if there is a gasoline-pow-ered generator anywhere in the vicinity, or if gasoline or propane is stored anywhere close by.*

In extreme circumstances, drain the engine oil and coolant, warm it, and replace it. Once again, it should not get too hot or else there will be a danger of cracking engine castings.

Improving Cranking Speed. Warming the battery (*not* with a propane torch, for heaven's sake) and engine oil will also improve cranking speeds. Engines with hand-cranks should be turned over manually a few times before cranking. When cranking with the starting motor, you can leave the decompression levers in the hand-crank position until the engine gains speed, and *then* disengage them.

DIESEL ENGINE CRANKS BUT DOES NOT START: QUICK REFERENCE

---

1. Preliminary Checks
1. Check that the fuel valve is open and the throttle advanced (p. 119).
2. Check that the cold start device is operative and substitute as necessary (p. 115).
3. Check the engine cranking speed and take steps to bring up to normal (p. 115).

2. If the engine still fails to start
1. Break an injector nut loose and check the fuel supply to the cylinders (p. 126). Change filters and bleed as necessary (pp. 120–126).
2. Remove the air filter and clean. Introduce some oil into the cylinders (p. 117).

Blocking the air intake with your hand during initial cranking with the starting motor reduces the volume of air entering the cylinders, lowers compression, and allows the engine to build up a little momentum. (*Never* do this with the engine running.) As soon as you remove your hand (while still continuing to crank), a full charge of air is drawn in, compression levels jump, and hopefully the engine fires. Disconnecting belt-driven auxiliary equipment (pumps, refrigeration compressors, and generators, but *not* alternators) will reduce the starting load on an engine.

At sea, some boats can be "bump started" by sailing with the propeller free-wheeling and then engaging forward gear while cranking. This is a useful way to assist a battery.

Starting fluid takes a toll on an engine. Starting fluid sprayed into the air inlet has a tendency to explode before a piston reaches the top of its stroke, severely stressing the engine. It should be used only as a last resort and extremely sparingly. Spray some on a handkerchief and hold it over the air inlet.

Improving Compression. There is little that can be done with leaking valves, but piston rings are another matter. On a cold engine, especially one that has not been run in a while, the film of lubricating oil that forms on pistons and cylinders when the engine is running tends to drain back down to the bottom of the engine. Then, when the engine is cranked, air escapes down the sides of the pistons. This is known as "blow-by."

If the engine is reluctant to fire, let it sit for a minute. Two things will happen. The unburned diesel in the cylinders will dribble down the cylinder walls and onto the top piston ring, and the battery will catch its breath. In the meantime, the heat of compression from the initial cranking will have taken some of the chill off the cylinders. Now hit the starter once again. The engine may well splutter into life.

If the engine still fails to fire, a small amount of oil introduced into the cylinders will dribble down onto the piston rings and seal them. This frequently has a dramatic effect on compression levels and may immediately cure starting difficulties.

How to get the oil into the cylinders? A few engines have little oil cups mounted on the top of the inlet manifold for this purpose. The cups are filled, and when the engine is cranked it sucks in the oil. Otherwise, remove the air filter and squirt oil into the manifolds as close to the cylinders as possible. If the engine is cranked while you squirt the oil, it will be carried in with the air stream.

On turbocharged engines, take care not to poke the tip of an oil can into the turbine blades. Expensive damage will result. On all engines, replace the air filter as soon as possible. It takes very little dirt to do serious damage to a diesel.

Use only a little oil, because a large amount will fill the cylinders and then damage pistons and connecting rods. When the engine fires, it will smoke abominably for a while, but will stop once the oil burns off. Don't neglect starting problems. Have a competent mechanic overhaul the engine at the first opportunity.

If the engine still fails to start it is time to look at the fuel system.

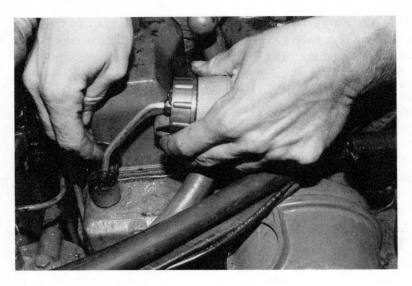

Oil cups on an inlet manifold (Sabb 2JZ).

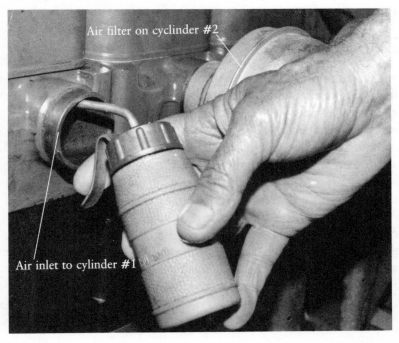

Squirting oil into the inlet manifold of a Volvo MD 17C.

Fuel Supply Problems

Preliminary Checks. The first thing to check is whether there is diesel in the tank and whether the fuel valve is open. The fuel suction line is invariably set off the bottom of the tank: If the level is low and the boat is heeling, the suction line may well be drawing in slugs of air as the fuel sloshes around.

The next thing to check is that the engine throttle is advanced. *If the throttle is closed it shuts off the fuel supply to the engine, which will then never start.* Some engines have a separate "kill" lever and cold-start device. These must be in their starting positions.

The engine should have a fuel filter with a glass bowl set close to the tank. This should be inspected for visual signs of water or dirt in the fuel. Evidence of either will necessitate changing filters and also bleeding the fuel system.

The Fuel System. When did you last change your fuel filters or check the tank for water and sedimentation? *Dirty fuel is the cause of up to 90 percent of marine diesel engine problems*! Most engines have two or three filters. The first in line from the fuel tank is (or should be) the filter with the glass bowl. Next is a screen filter in the top of the fuel lift pump (feed pump), which draws the diesel from the tank and passes it on to the injection system. This screen is easily accessible by undoing the screw in the center of the lift pump and removing the cover.

From the lift pump, we come to the secondary filter, which is always mounted somewhere on the engine itself. Nowadays, this is often a spin-on filter. Otherwise, one central bolt loosens the filter body, providing access to a replaceable paper element.

If the filters are dirty, they should be changed and then reinspected just a few running hours after changing. A contaminated batch of fuel may have been taken on board, in which case the filters will need changing repeatedly until the contamination clears up. Any boat going offshore should carry a batch of spare filters. At the first opportunity, the fuel tank needs draining and flushing.

From the secondary filter, the fuel is passed to an injection pump—a solid little unit with a number of small pipes leading

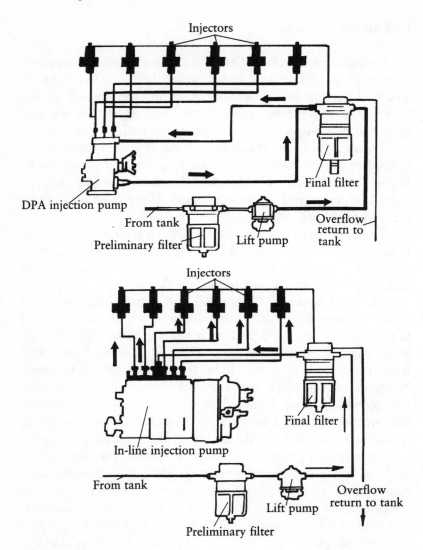

Fuel schematics for a distributor injection pump (top) *and an in-line jerk pump* (bottom). *(Courtesy Lucas CAV)*

from it to each cylinder. Each cylinder has an injector (atomiser), either screwed into the top of the engine or held down by a plate and a couple of bolts. Injectors have two pipes attached to them—the injection line coming from the injection pump, and a "leak-off" pipe, which allows excess fuel to drain back to the top of the secondary filter or directly to the fuel tank.

Injection lines and leak-off pipes are easily distinguished. The former run as individual pipes from the injection pump to the injectors. Leak-off pipes are all tied together from one injector running to the next and use a common return line to the filter or tank.

Bleeding a Fuel System. Diesel engines just will not run with air in the fuel supply. Anytime the engine runs out of fuel,

Lift pump strainer.

or the filters are changed, or a leak develops between the fuel
tank and the lift pump, the fuel system has to be purged of all
air, a process known as "bleeding."

Between the lift pump and the injectors are one or more
bleed screws or nipples. On the base of the lift pump is a handle
for manual operation. (Engines that do not have the type of lift
pump illustrated will have a manual pump tacked onto one of
the filters or the injection pump.)

If the bleed nipples are loosened (not removed) and the lift
pump is operated manually, fuel will be pumped out of the

*To clean the gauze strainer in the lift pump: (1) Remove
the cover and joint from the top of the fuel lift pump and
remove the gauze strainer. (2) Carefully wash any sediment
from the lift pump. (3) Clean the gauze strainer, joint, and
cover. (4) Assemble the lift pump. Ensure that a good joint is
made between the lift pump body and the cover because any
leakage here will let air into the fuel system. (Courtesy Perkins
Engines Ltd)*

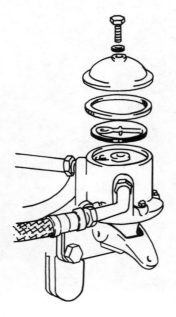

nipples. If the lift pump will not operate, turn the engine over a revolution to free up the pump mechanism. The idea is to start at the bleed point closest to the lift pump (generally on the secondary filter), to pump fuel out of this nipple until it runs *completely free of all air bubbles,* and then to tighten it down and move onto the next bleed point in line (generally on the fuel injection pump).

Some filters do not have bleed points, in which case it will be necessary to loosen the fuel lines—first the inlet and then the outlet. Some fuel pumps have two bleed points, the lower of which should be bled first.

The injection pump should now have a supply of clean, air-free diesel. To bleed the injection lines up to the injectors, set *the throttle wide open.* Often all that is needed is to crank the engine for up to 30 seconds, but no more—the starter may overheat and be damaged.

Bleeding a secondary filter. (Courtesy Perkins Engines)

Bleeding a fuel inlet to an injection pump. (Courtesy Perkins Engines)

Bleeding the lower nipple on a CAV DPA distributor pump. (Courtesy Perkins Engines)

Bleeding the upper nipple on a CAV DPA distributor pump. (Courtesy Perkins Engines)

Injector nuts, Volvo MD 17C.

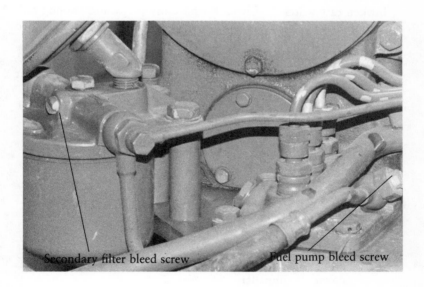

Bleed points, Volvo MD 17C.

If the engine still does not start, one or more of the nuts holding the injection lines to the injectors should be loosened. When the engine is turned over a few more times, a tiny drop of fuel should spurt from each connection at the injection stroke for that cylinder, on every second revolution of the engine. If no fuel comes out, or if there is air in the fuel, the engine has been bled inadequately and it will be necessary to start at the beginning again.

DIESEL ENGINE OVERHEATS: QUICK REFERENCE

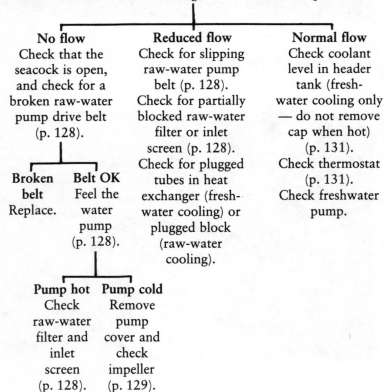

Check the raw-water discharge from the exhaust (p. 128).

No flow
Check that the seacock is open, and check for a broken raw-water pump drive belt (p. 128).

Broken belt
Replace.

Belt OK
Feel the water pump (p. 128).

Pump hot
Check raw-water filter and inlet screen (p. 128).

Pump cold
Remove pump cover and check impeller (p. 129).

Reduced flow
Check for slipping raw-water pump belt (p. 128).
Check for partially blocked raw-water filter or inlet screen (p. 128).
Check for plugged tubes in heat exchanger (fresh-water cooling) or plugged block (raw-water cooling).

Normal flow
Check coolant level in header tank (fresh-water cooling only — do not remove cap when hot) (p. 131).
Check thermostat (p. 131).
Check freshwater pump.

Operating Problems

Common problems that occur when the engine is running include overheating, low oil pressure, and misfiring.

Overheating

One of the first things to check is the oil level (see Low Oil Pressure below). To go further, however, we must distinguish between raw-water cooled engines and those cooled with fresh water. Raw-water cooling circulates seawater directly through the engine; freshwater-cooled engines have a closed system, like an automobile's, but in place of a radiator there is a header tank to keep the system topped up, and a heat exchanger—a cylinder with a mass of small tubes running through it. Engine cooling water circulates through the body of the cylinder while seawater is pumped through the tubes, carrying off the engine heat. The seawater is then passed overboard via the exhaust.

Raw-water cooling.

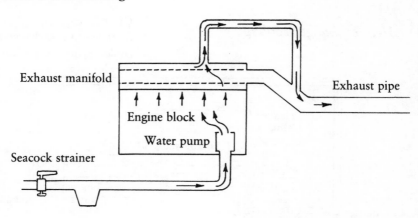

Freshwater-cooled engines thus have two cooling circuits—the engine circuit and the raw water—and two water pumps, as opposed to the one found on raw-water cooled engines.

Raw-water circuits.   Faced with overheating:

• Cut back the engine throttle.
• Check the exhaust to see whether water is being expelled at the normal rate. If it is (and 90 percent of the time it won't be), troubleshooting procedures beyond the scope of this book are needed.
• If water is not coming out the exhaust normally, check the water pump, which is mounted on the front of the engine, slightly down and off to one side, for a broken or slipping drive belt. Tighten or replace if necessary.
• If the pump is turning, shut off the engine and feel the pump body to see if it is hot, or even warm. If it is, the pump is running dry and the impeller is in imminent danger of tearing up. Note: if the impeller has already failed, the pump may have already cooled down and will give no external clues that it has failed.

Raw-Water Strainer and Inlet Screen. A failure of the raw-water circuit is almost always due to a blockage of the seawater

Heat exchanger cooling.

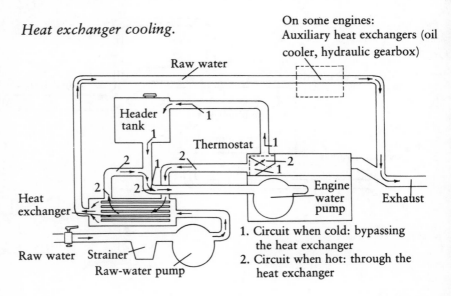

On some engines:
Auxiliary heat exchangers (oil cooler, hydraulic gearbox)

1. Circuit when cold: bypassing the heat exchanger
2. Circuit when hot: through the heat exchanger

intake, perhaps induced by forgetting to open the intake's sea-cock! The seawater intake will be set way down in the hull and should have some kind of a screen over it. The only way to see if a plastic bag is stuck over the screen is to dive down or to open up the raw-water circuit at some point below sea level inside the boat and make sure that there is a good flow. How-ever, with the engine shut down, any trash stuck to the screen may wash off and float away.

If the boat has no inlet screen, inspect the raw-water filter. This should be close by the seacock and will have a glass bowl with a removable screen inside it. If this coarse-meshed screen is clogged with bits of flotsam, you may have found the problem.

Raw-Water Pump. If you still find no explanation for a complete failure of the raw-water circuit, check the pump

Raw-water filter.

impeller. Raw-water pumps are almost universally made by Jabsco, and all have covers held in place with six screws. With the cover off, the impeller is clearly visible. All its blades (vanes) should be intact. If they are, turn the engine over to make sure that the impeller is actually turning and not slipping on its shaft.

Raw-water pump.

Impeller-type pump. To service, remove end cover and gasket. Pull impeller out by grasping hub with pliers. Replace impeller, gasket, and end cover. A light coating of grease in impeller bore will aid priming on dry startup. Standard gasket is 0.010 inch thick. (Courtesy Jabsco Pumps)

If the impeller blades are stripped off, pull out what's left with a pair of needlenose pliers or pry it out with two screwdrivers. A few impellers are locked in place with a set screw, but most slide right out. Some are fitted with keys, which you may lose if you're not careful. A spare impeller should *always* be carried on board and is pushed into place, bending the blades down in the appropriate direction for the rotation of the pump. (Blade tips are bent counterclockwise for clockwise rotation, and clockwise for counterclockwise rotation.)

Next, track down the broken blades from the old impeller. Should it not be possible to find them all, take apart the cooling system at the earliest opportunity and account for all the missing pieces.

One final point on the raw-water side. If oil is present in the raw-water discharge (the exhaust will be making a slick), the cooling tubes in either the engine or gearbox heat exchanger may have corroded through. This is an unfortunately common occurrence due to the use of galvanically noncompatible materials in cheap coolers and poor onboard electrical circuits. The engine will have to be shut down until a new oil cooler can be fitted, unless there are adequate hoses and connections on board to bypass the oil side of the cooler. In this case the engine can be run at a reduced load, keeping a close eye on its water temperature and oil pressure (or the gearbox temperature). The oil may need changing before restarting if any water has found its way into the engine (or gearbox). The water side of the cooler can be bypassed or left in place with the disconnected oil fittings plugged off.

Thermostats. Thermostat failures are discussed under Freshwater Circuits below.

Freshwater Circuits. Freshwater circuits are far less prone to trouble. The most obvious reason for overheating is a low water level. Check the header tank, but just as with a radiator, *never remove the cap when hot.* The contents will be under pressure and can cause serious burns.

Thermostats. Thermostats on both raw- and freshwater-cooled engines malfunction from time to time. Older engines tend to have bellows-type thermostats, which will fail in the *open* position, giving too much cooling rather than too little. Nearly all modern engines have wax-filled thermostats that fail in the *closed* position, causing the engine to overheat.

Thermostats are generally found in a bell-shaped housing toward the front and top of the engine, and will almost certainly be associated with a cooling hose or two. If the thermostat is suspect, by all means pull it out. Running without one for a while will do the engine no harm. To test the thermostat, put it in a pot of cold water and heat it. If it opens before the water boils, it's almost certainly operative.

Low Oil Pressure

Anytime an engine heats up, oil pressure will fall as the oil becomes less viscous. However, *insufficient or dirty oil may be the real cause of the overheating.*

Thermostat housing on a Volvo MD 17C.

Thermostat removed from a Volvo MD 17C.

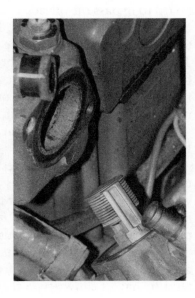

Low Oil Level.   The oil in an engine plays a vital role in cooling internal surfaces and bearings. A low oil level will cause the small amount remaining to heat up excessively, and if left for too long, will lead to piston and bearing seizure. Any kind of a seizure generates a tremendous amount of additional friction and heat.

A sixth of all bearing failures in engines are due to a lack of oil. Faced with either overheating or low oil pressure, check the oil dipstick, and add oil as needed.

Dirty Oil.   An even sadder statistic is that *over 40 percent of all bearing failures are from dirty oil.* Failure to carry out regular oil change procedures rarely leads to a sudden crisis. A gradual loss of pressure and slowly rising temperatures may be the only clues to greatly accelerated engine wear. When a major mechanical failure does occur, such as a seized piston or wiped-out bearing, nothing can be done to fix it at sea.

Misfiring and Smoke

If a motor runs erratically on initial startup, quite possibly accompanied by little puffs of white smoke out of the exhaust, the culprit is almost certainly low compression in one or more cylinders. The misfiring should clear up as the motor warms up, but the engine needs professional help to solve the compression problem. When the same symptoms occur in an already warm engine that has been running OK, the culprit is almost certainly water in the fuel supply, or else the engine is running out of diesel. Black smoke indicates overloading (perhaps a rope wrapped around the propeller?), an obstruction in the air supply (a dirty filter or defective turbocharger?), or improper injection (the result of dirty fuel?). Turbochargers and fuel injectors are off-limits to the weekend mechanic. Propellers, air filters, and fuel systems can all be checked as previously outlined.

6

Troubleshooting Inboard Gasoline Engines

Inboard gasoline engines differ in two major respects from diesels: The fuel supply is drawn in with the inlet air (as opposed to being injected into the cylinder), and the compression ratios are much lower, which means that a separate ignition system is required to set off the compressed fuel/air mixture. We thus have a carburetor, spark plugs, coils, and all the other paraphernalia associated with gas engines, and herein lies 90 percent of their problems.

Warning! *Gasoline vapors are heavier than air and highly explosive. Any gas leaks, drips, or spills tend to accumulate in the bilges of a boat, and then it takes only one tiny spark to cause an explosion. Many of the following test procedures involve creating such a spark. Always clean up all spills, keep the engine room vented, and check and doublecheck that there is not a trace of gasoline vapor in the air before carrying out these tests. Get down on your hands and knees and get your nose as deep in the bilge as possible.*

Carburetion— General Principles

A carburetor has a bowl (the *float bowl*) filled with gas, with a small tube (a *jet*) leading to a restriction in the air intake (the *venturi*). As air rushes through the venturi it sucks gas out of

FIXED-CHOKE CARBURETOR OPERATION

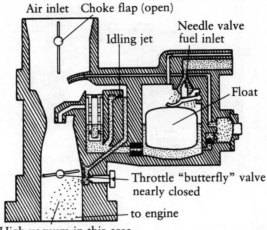

When idling, the high vacuum on the engine side of the butter-fly valve draws fuel through the low speed (idle) jet.

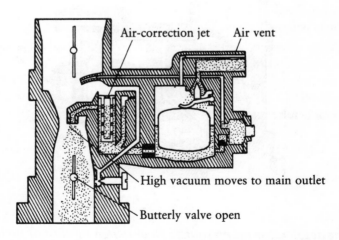

When the butterfly valve is opened, fuel is drawn from the main jet as the vacuum around it increases.

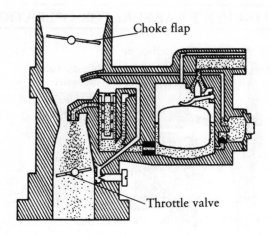

Choke flap

Throttle valve

A flap is used to partially block the barrel for cold starts. It increases vacuum around the fuel outlet and draws more fuel to provide a rich mixture.

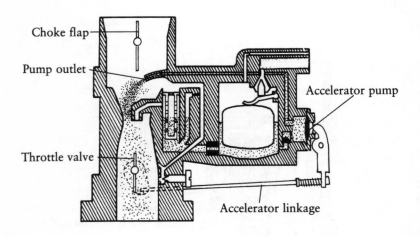

Choke flap

Pump outlet

Accelerator pump

Throttle valve

Accelerator linkage

The accelerator pump squirts an enrichening shot of fuel down the barrel to provide a quick response when the throttle is opened quickly.

the jet, carrying it into the engine. The float bowl has a hinged float pressing against a needle valve. As the level of gas in the bowl is lowered, the float drops, the needle valve opens, and the fuel pump refills the bowl.

Engine speed is controlled by a butterfly valve, a hinged flap more or less blocking the engine air intake. When the flap is closed, little fuel/air mixture can be sucked into the engine. When it is open, the mixture flows freely.

At low engine speeds, the engine is pulling against the restriction imposed by the butterfly, creating considerable suction. A small jet placed on the *engine* side of the butterfly valve supplies fuel at idle speeds. This is the "low speed" or "idle" jet. When the butterfly valve opens, the main jet in the venturi takes over.

Excess fuel for cold starting is provided by placing a second butterfly valve, called a *choke,* at the inlet of the carburetor. When this is closed, the engine pulls a vacuum in the whole carburetor, greatly increasing the volume of fuel sucked out of the main jet. Excess fuel for rapid acceleration is provided by an *accelerator pump,* a piston or diaphragm in a cylinder of fuel that pumps gas into the venturi in response to any sudden movement of the throttle.

The carburetor just described is called a "fixed choke." Another design, the "variable choke," does away with the idle jet and choke. A "compound" or "dual throat" carburetor has two or more fixed-choke carburetors in one unit. They are easily identified when the air filter is removed by their two or more inlets ("barrels") with a choke in each one. One barrel has a low-speed jet; the other has a high-speed jet that cuts in when the engine accelerates beyond a certain point.

For basic troubleshooting, it is necessary to identify the throttle linkage to the butterfly valve, the choke(s), the float chamber, and the jets (with their external adjusting screws, if fitted). Also, locate the fuel filter attached somewhere in the fuel line. Fuel pumps are either mechanical diaphragm pumps, as on most diesels, or electric solenoid pumps.

VARIABLE-CHOKE CARBURETOR OPERATION

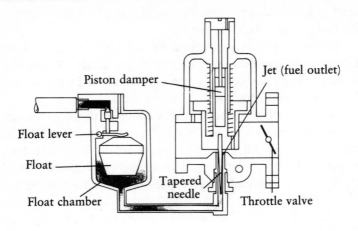

Piston damper

Jet (fuel outlet)

Float lever

Float

Float chamber

Tapered needle

Throttle valve

As with the fixed-jet carburetor, the float chamber supplies fuel at the correct level to the outlet. The piston controls the air flow and a tapered needle meters the flow of fuel.

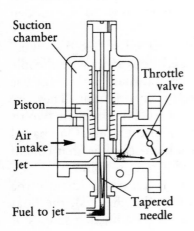

Suction chamber

Throttle valve

Piston

Air intake

Jet

Fuel to jet

Tapered needle

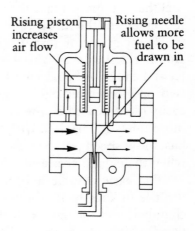

Rising piston increases air flow

Rising needle allows more fuel to be drawn in

Throttle shut: Lack of vacuum in the barrel allows the piston to fall, restricting mixture flow.

Throttle open: Engine vacuum lifts the piston, providing an increased flow of fuel and air.

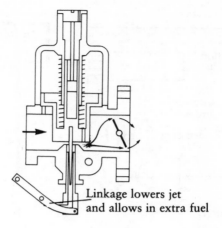

Linkage lowers jet
and allows in extra fuel

Cold starting: Operating the choke lowers the jet, allowing more fuel to be drawn into the barrel.

Ignition—General Principles

The ignition system on a gasoline engine has to provide a spark of up to 25,000 volts at a very precisely timed moment. There are three crucial components: the coil, the contact breaker (CB), and the distributor.

A coil has a primary winding of a few turns of heavy wire surrounded by a secondary winding of thousands of turns of tiny wire. Voltage is fed from the battery, through the ignition switch and the primary winding to a contact breaker, then back to the battery, energizing the primary winding. This completes the *low-tension (LT)* circuit of the ignition system. At precise moments, the contact breaker opens, cutting this circuit, and this causes the coil to generate a very high voltage in its secondary winding.

This high voltage is fed into the distributor (generally mounted on top of the contact breaker) and down to a rotating arm (the *rotor arm*). Inside the distributor is a terminal for each cylinder on the engine. The rotor arm lines up the high

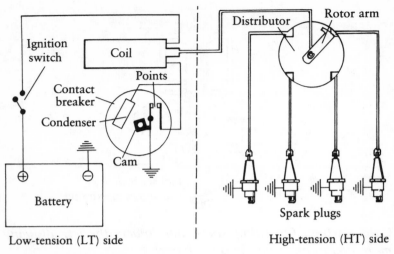

Ignition circuit schematic.

voltage with the appropriate cylinder at the appropriate time, and feeds it to the relevant spark plug. This completes the *high-tension (HT)* circuit.

Electronic Ignition

When the contact breaker opens, a spark occurs across its *points* —the two pieces of metal that actually make and break the electrical circuit. To reduce points erosion, a condenser (capacitor) is included in the circuit on conventional ignition systems. The condenser stores electricity momentarily as the points open, thus reducing the arcing, but there is still some arcing at the points. *Capacitor discharge (CD)* electronic ignition uses the points to trigger a switch, which then makes and breaks the circuit, thus eliminating arcing at the points.

Modern electronic ignitions use a light beam or magnetic switch to break the low-tension circuit, thus doing away with the points, so there is nothing to maintain or adjust. Even more advanced ignition units dispense with the rotor arm and distribute the high-tension voltage to the spark plugs electronically. These engines have a separate coil for each cylinder. Once again, there is nothing on the electronic side to maintain or adjust.

The following procedures assume a mechanical ignition system. With electronic ignition, the reader will have to abstract whatever parts are still relevant.

Failure to Start

If a motor refuses to crank, or is sluggish, refer to the relevant sections in Chapter Five.

Flooding. If an engine has been cranked a good bit but refuses to fire, it is quite likely flooded. Move the throttle *slowly* to its wide open position. If there is a manual choke, open it wide. An automatic choke can be opened by removing the air filter and holding it open. Do not force it. Allow the engine to sit for a minute or so to vaporize excess fuel, then crank again. If it fires and dies, it probably now needs a little choke. If it still fails to fire, it is time to do some troubleshooting.

Basic Troubleshooting. The immediate objective is to decide if we have an ignition or carburetion problem. Remove a high-tension lead from a spark plug, slide back its rubber sleeve to expose the terminal (or else slip a nail or something similar into the terminal), and hold the terminal (or nail) 1/4 inch from a good ground, such as a clean spot on the engine block (but not anywhere near the carburetor!). Crank the engine. A healthy spark (blue and crackling!) should jump from the terminal to the block.

Given a good spark, we almost certainly have a carburetion problem, fouled plugs, or both. If there is no spark, we definitely have an ignition problem.

Ignition Fault Finding

First, determine whether the problem is in the high-tension or low-tension circuit. Pull out the HT lead coming out of the center of the coil, hold it an eighth of an inch from its socket, and crank the engine (Test 1). No spark indicates a problem in the coil or LT side. A spark narrows down the problem to the distributor or HT leads.

**GASOLINE ENGINE CRANKS BUT FAILS TO FIRE:
QUICK REFERENCE**

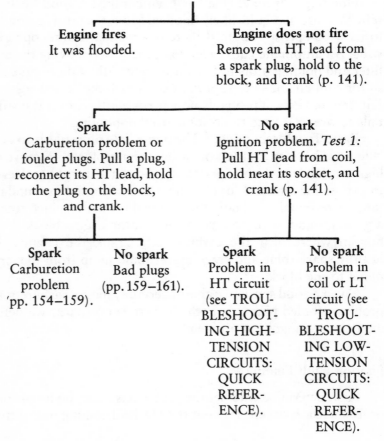

Open the choke, put the throttle slowly to its wide-open position, wait a minute, and crank (p. 141).

Engine fires
It was flooded.

Engine does not fire
Remove an HT lead from a spark plug, hold to the block, and crank (p. 141).

Spark
Carburetion problem or fouled plugs. Pull a plug, reconnect its HT lead, hold the plug to the block, and crank.

No spark
Ignition problem. *Test 1:* Pull HT lead from coil, hold near its socket, and crank (p. 141).

Spark
Carburetion problem
'pp. 154–159).

No spark
Bad plugs
(pp. 159–161).

Spark
Problem in HT circuit (see TROUBLESHOOTING HIGH-TENSION CIRCUITS: QUICK REFERENCE).

No spark
Problem in coil or LT circuit (see TROUBLESHOOTING LOW-TENSION CIRCUITS: QUICK REFERENCE).

Low-tension Circuit (Refer to Quick-Reference Chart).
It helps enormously when troubleshooting a low-tension circuit
to have a test lamp. These cost about $6 and have a plastic
handle with a bulb inside and a metal probe, which is touched
to the terminal to be tested. A wire with a "crocodile clip"
attached to any convenient ground (earth) completes the circuit.

General Test. To make a quick test of the LT side, remove
the distributor cap and rotor to expose the contact breaker,
and turn the engine over until the contact points are closed. (It
is difficult to do this with the starting motor. If the engine does
not have a hand crank, turn it manually by placing a wrench
over the nut that holds the crankshaft pulley on, or by putting
the engine in gear and placing a pipe wrench on the propeller
shaft. Make sure the ignition switch is *off,* and that you turn

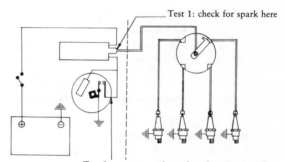

Test 1: check for spark here

Test 2: connect test lamp from here to ground

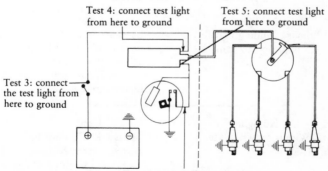

Test 4: connect test light
from here to ground

Test 5: connect test light
from here to ground

Test 3: connect
the test light from
here to ground

Tests 3, 4, 5, 6: disconnect this wire.
For test 6, connect the test light between
this wire and ground.

TROUBLESHOOTING LOW-TENSION CIRCUITS: QUICK REFERENCE

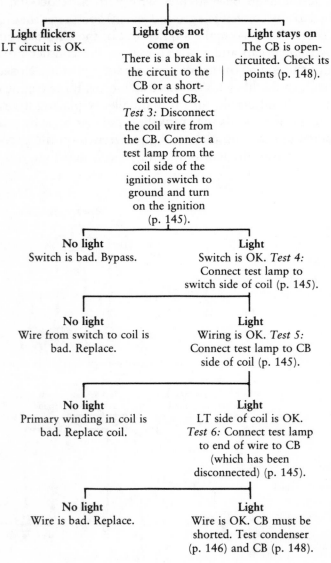

Test 2: Connect a test lamp from the coil terminal on the contact breaker (CB) to ground and crank (p. 145).

Light flickers
LT circuit is OK.

Light does not come on
There is a break in the circuit to the CB or a short-circuited CB.
Test 3: Disconnect the coil wire from the CB. Connect a test lamp from the coil side of the ignition switch to ground and turn on the ignition (p. 145).

Light stays on
The CB is open-circuited. Check its points (p. 148).

No light
Switch is bad. Bypass.

Light
Switch is OK. *Test 4:* Connect test lamp to switch side of coil (p. 145).

No light
Wire from switch to coil is bad. Replace.

Light
Wiring is OK. *Test 5:* Connect test lamp to CB side of coil (p. 145).

No light
Primary winding in coil is bad. Replace coil.

Light
LT side of coil is OK.
Test 6: Connect test lamp to end of wire to CB (which has been disconnected) (p. 145).

No light
Wire is bad. Replace.

Light
Wire is OK. CB must be shorted. Test condenser (p. 146) and CB (p. 148).

the engine in its normal direction of rotation.) Switch on the ignition, and gently separate the points by pushing on the spring-loaded side with a screwdriver. Note: Do not make a connection across the points with the screwdriver. (If the unit has two sets of points, the second set will need to be wedged open with a piece of plastic or cardboard for this test to work.) If a small spark jumps across the points, the LT circuit is working. A large spark may show a faulty condenser.

Troubleshooting with the Test Lamp. The best place to start testing the LT circuit is at the connection on the outside of the contact breaker unit where the LT wire coming from the coil is attached. Connect the crocodile clip on the test lamp to ground, hold the probe tip to the contact breaker terminal, and crank the engine (Test 2). One of three things will happen: The light will flicker on and off, which indicates the LT circuit is working; the light will not come on, which shows a break in the supply to the contact breaker or a short circuit in the contact breaker itself; or the light will stay on, which tells us that the contact breaker is not working. (See Contact Breaker Operations below.)

Switch Test. If the tester doesn't light, disconnect the wire from the coil to the contact breaker and place it where the loose end will not ground out. (Leave it disconnected for the next four tests.) Connect the test lamp crocodile clip to ground and touch the probe to the *coil* side of the *ignition switch* (Test 3). Turn on the ignition. The tester should light up. If it does not, the switch or its wiring is bad.

Coil Test (LT Side). If the tester lights, move to the *switch* side of the *coil* (Test 4). No light means the wiring to the coil is bad and must be replaced. If the tester lights, move to the other side of the *coil* (Test 5). No light means the primary winding in the coil is out and the coil needs replacing. If the tester lights, move to the end of the wire leading to the contact breaker, the wire disconnected earlier (Test 6). No light means the wire is bad and should be replaced. If the tester lights, the circuit to this point is working, so the contact breaker itself must be shorted. At this point, reconnect the wire from the coil to the contact breaker.

Contact Breaker Operation. We have now established that we have either a shorted contact breaker or one that is permanently open-circuited (the light stays on all the time when conducting Test 2). The contact breaker has one point mounted on a base plate that is connected to the ground. The other point pivots on an *insulated* pin on the base plate. This point is spring loaded with a plastic heel (the breaker arm rubbing block or "cam follower") which rests against an eccentric shaft—the rotor drive shaft. As the shaft turns it moves the rubbing block in and out, which opens and closes the points. The shaft has as many corners (cams) as there are cylinders on the engine.

Contact breaker unit. The contact breaker is the low-voltage part of the distributor. Here are situated the contact-breaker points, which time the ignition; and the condenser, which prevents excessive arcing at the points.

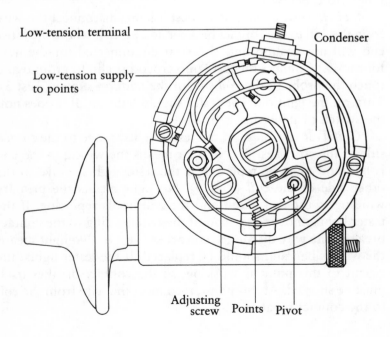

Low-tension terminal

Condenser

Low-tension supply to points

Adjusting screw   Points   Pivot

Contact Breaker Short Circuit and Condenser Tests. A short circuit can arise in the contact breaker from:

- Points failing to open, generally as a result of the plastic heel wearing down where it rubs on the cams.
- Frayed, stray, or loose wires grounding out.
- Improper installation of the points, leaving out the plastic insulators that keep the two points electrically separated.

Distributor and contact breaker. The distributor allocates high-voltage pulses to the spark plugs in the correct firing order by means of a rotor arm. The arm is usually driven by the engine camshaft. The contact breaker interrupts the low-tension current flow. A cam on a rotating shaft determines whether the two points of the contact breaker are in contact, and therefore whether current is allowed to pass through them. One point is fixed; the other is operated by the cam.

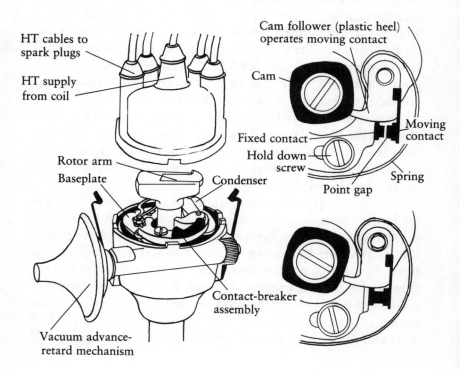

HT cables to spark plugs

HT supply from coil

Rotor arm

Baseplate

Vacuum advance-retard mechanism

Condenser

Contact-breaker assembly

Cam follower (plastic heel) operates moving contact

Cam

Fixed contact

Hold down screw

Moving contact

Spring

Point gap

Occasionally, a condenser will short-circuit. To test one, unscrew it from the contact breaker but leave its wire connected. Hook the test lamp between its case and a good ground and turn on the ignition. If the tester lights, the condenser is shorted out and must be replaced. If the condenser has two wires, leave the one to the points connected, disconnect the ground wire, and connect the tester between it and ground. A quick test of a condenser can be made by disconnecting it from the circuit and cranking the engine. If the motor now fires, the condenser is shorted. The engine must be shut back down immediately. If it is run without a condenser, the points will rapidly burn away.

Contact Breaker Open Circuit. A permanently open-circuited contact breaker is likely to be the result of too wide a points gap (see below) or a buildup of corrosion and pitting on the points until they fail to make a circuit.

Contact Breaker Points Servicing. Turn the engine over until one of the cams on the rotor shaft has the points open to their maximum extent. The engine can be turned with a wrench on the crankshaft pulley nut or by putting it in gear and turning the propeller shaft. The points should be clean and free from pitting. If at all corroded, they need replacing. As a temporary measure, they can be taken out and "dressed up" (cleaned) with a file. A nail file will work.

Points are removed by undoing the one central hold-down screw in the base plate, and they come out as a set mounted on the plate. It is essential when replacing them to refit all the various insulating washers in their correct locations, or the contact breaker will short out.

The points gap is very important for engine operation. It is set at the moment of maximum opening. With the points in place, loosen the hold-down screw and ease the points open or shut as necessary by turning the adjusting screw or, if one is not fitted, by twisting a screwdriver between the base plate and the side of the contact breaker housing. Retighten the retaining screw and doublecheck the gap, which will be specified in the engine manual. It is usually .015 to .020 inch (0.38 to 0.50 mm) and can only be properly measured with feeler gauges. If

---

TROUBLESHOOTING HIGH-TENSION CIRCUITS:
QUICK REFERENCE

Test 1: Put HT lead back in coil (if still out from earlier tests), remove other end from distributor cap, hold to the block, and crank (p. 149).

Weak Spark	**Good Spark**	**No Spark**
Test the condenser (p. 146).	*Test 2:* Replace the HT lead in the distributor, pull a plug lead from the distributor, hold close to its socket, and crank (p. 150).	Defective HT lead from coil to distributor, or defective coil. Replace coil and lead.

No Spark	**Spark**
Distributor is bad. Remove the cap (p. 152). Check for dirt, cracks, and moisture. Clean the central electrode, rotor arm terminal, and spark plug terminals. Spray liberally with WD 40.	HT leads to plugs or plugs themselves are bad. Replace plug lead in distributor, pull HT leads one by one from plugs, hold to a ground, and crank.

No Spark	**Spark**
HT leads are bad. Replace.	Plugs are bad. Pull and inspect (p. 159).

these are not available, a gap about the thickness of a thumbnail will get one home.

High-Tension Circuit (Refer to Quick Reference Chart). If the original test indicated a problem in the HT circuit, put the HT lead that was removed back in the coil, pull its other end out of the distributor cap, hold it ¼ inch from a good ground, and check for a spark (Test 1). This can be done by cranking the engine or by turning over the engine until the points are closed, switching on the ignition, and prying the points apart. A clear blue spark should jump to ground. A weak or yellow spark may show a defective condenser (see above). No spark indicates a failure in the secondary windings of the coil or the HT lead itself. Replace both.

Testing the Distributor and Plug Leads. If a good spark is present, the problem is either with the distributor or the plug

A rotor arm, turned by the engine, distributes HT current from the coil to each spark plug in turn.

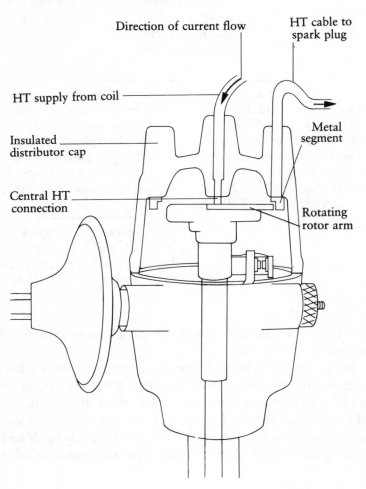

Direction of current flow

HT cable to spark plug

HT supply from coil

Metal segment

Insulated distributor cap

Central HT connection

Rotating rotor arm

leads. With the rotor arm, distributor cap, and plug leads all in place, pull a plug lead from the distributor cap, hold it close to its socket, and crank the engine (Test 2). No spark means the distributor is defective, while a spark indicates defective plug leads or plugs.

Distributor cap and plug leads on an Atomic 4 gas engine.

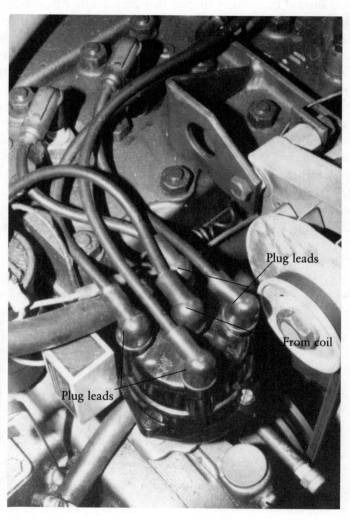

Cleaning a Distributor and Rotor Arm. Distributor caps are held in place with a couple of spring clips or screws, which need only half a turn to release. Inspect the cap for dampness, dirt, or cracks, any of which will allow the HT voltage to run to ground. Check the terminals inside the cap for corrosion, and clean as necessary.

The cap will have a spring-loaded carbon rod ("brush") or metal plate that bears down on the center of the rotor arm. There should be a shiny spot at this point. The rotor itself can be lifted out by pulling straight up on it—there is no need to note its position as it can only go back one way. Thoroughly clean and dry the cap and its terminals and give them a shot of WD 40. Many times, this is all that is needed to get an engine going.

Ignition Timing. Under normal circumstances, there is no reason for ignition timing to change enough to prevent starting. It should be checked only *after the points gap has been correctly set.* Trace the HT lead from the spark plug on the cylinder at the front of the engine down to the distributor cap. Mark its position in relation to the base of the distributor, then remove the cap. Turn the engine over until the rotor lines up with the mark you made on the distributor—the piston on this

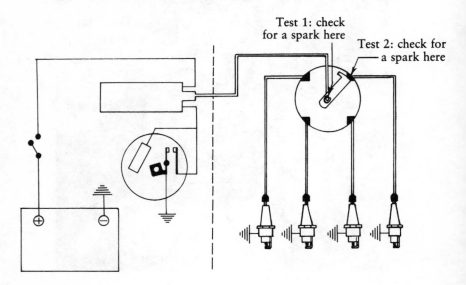

cylinder (#1) will now be more or less at the top of its compression stroke (assuming that the timing has not been completely altered, and there should be no reason for it to have been). *It is essential to have the rotor line up with the correct point on the distributor or else the timing will get thoroughly messed up, so do this with some care.*

On the crankshaft pulley (at the bottom and center of the engine) or on the flywheel will be a series of marks indicating Top Dead Center (TDC) for this piston, and various degrees of rotation Before Top Dead Center (BTDC). Somewhere on the block or flywheel housing will be a small pointer.

Ignition timing is either "static" (done with the engine stopped) or "dynamic" (with the engine running). Static timing, which is what we are doing, is generally 5 to 8 degrees BTDC. (Check the engine manual. If this is not available, assume 8 degrees.)

Timing marks on different engines.

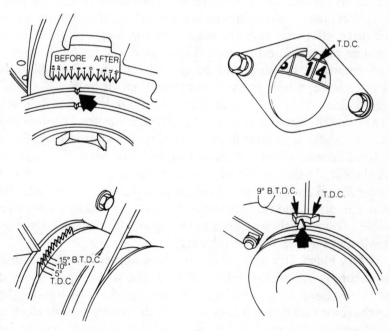

Connect the test light from the LT terminal on the *contact breaker side of the coil* to ground and manually rock the engine backward and forward with the ignition on. The light should go on and off. Back the engine up until the light goes out and then slowly turn it forward. The moment the light first comes on is when the points open, and the timing marks should line up. If not, the distributor body must be rotated slightly. First line up the engine timing marks (by turning the engine) and then rotate the distributor to find the point at which the light first comes on. This is done either with a knurled knob on the side of the distributor or by loosening a clamp at its base and turning it by hand. Tighten the clamp and doublecheck the timing by rocking the engine as before.

Carburetion Fault Finding

First pull the spark plugs (noting which cylinders they come from) and see if they are wet (and smell of gas) or dry.

Wet Plugs.   Wet plugs indicate flooding. If extremely sooty or dirty, they may not fire at all. Dry the plugs, clean them as best as possible, and replace. The engine will probably fire.

Persistent flooding can be caused by a filthy air filter, a stuck choke, a hole in the carburetor float (if hollow), a saturated float (if solid), or an incorrect float level (see below). Take out the float as described under Carburetor Dismantling below. Shake a hollow float to see if there is liquid in it. Place a solid float in a bowl of gas—it should float high. If it doesn't, replace it. At the same time, check the needle valve for signs of wear (for example, a "step" on the valve face). To test, hold the valve in place and blow in the fuel inlet—no leakage is permissible. You probably will not have a spare, but fortunately, this malfunction is unlikely to occur.

Dry Plugs. Dry plugs indicate a lack of fuel. Check the tank and supply valve. Assuming we have gas, we want to know if it is reaching the carburetor. Disconnect the fuel line at the carburetor and direct it into a can. If the motor has an electric fuel pump, turning on the ignition should cause gas to be

TROUBLESHOOTING CARBURETION: QUICK REFERENCE

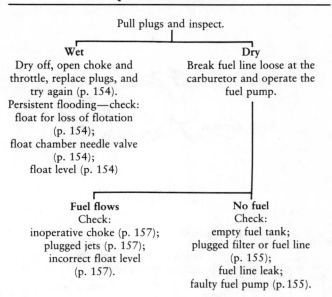

Pull plugs and inspect.

Wet
Dry off, open choke and throttle, replace plugs, and try again (p. 154).
Persistent flooding—check:
float for loss of flotation (p. 154);
float chamber needle valve (p. 154);
float level (p. 154)

Dry
Break fuel line loose at the carburetor and operate the fuel pump.

Fuel flows
Check:
inoperative choke (p. 157);
plugged jets (p. 157);
incorrect float level (p. 157).

No fuel
Check:
empty fuel tank;
plugged filter or fuel line (p. 155);
fuel line leak;
faulty fuel pump (p. 155).

pumped out. To check a mechanical fuel pump, the engine will have to be cranked, manually or with the starting motor.

Fuel Pump. No fuel may be the result of a plugged filter or line, or a fuel pump failure. On an electric pump, connect the test lamp from the positive side of the pump (connected to the battery) to a good ground and turn on the ignition. If it lights, the pump has juice. If it doesn't, suspect a fault in the ignition circuit between battery and pump. Assuming electricity is going to the pump, place the test lamp between the ground terminal of the pump and a good ground. If it lights, there is a fault in the ground wire: Clean the terminals or replace the wire. If it fails to light, the pump is bad. Sometimes a good smart tap on a pump body with a wrench will kick it into action. If this fails, remove the end cover and check its points for corrosion and burning. Clean them as you would the points on the contact breaker.

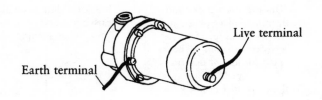

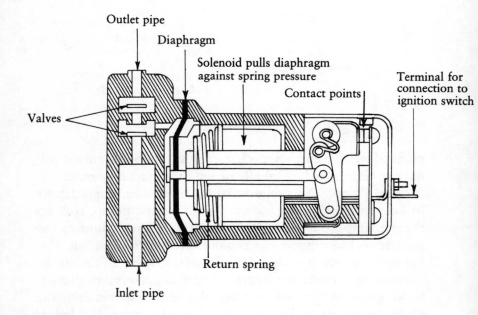

Electric fuel pump. This pump uses a solenoid to operate its diaphragm.

If the carburetor has fuel, check the choke to see that it is closing. If it is, the number one candidate for trouble is a blocked jet. Remove the air filter and throttle linkage (make a sketch of it if you're at all unsure how to put it back), disconnect the fuel line, and take the top off the carburetor (or drop the float bowl, depending on the carburetor).

Carburetor Dismantling

Fixed-choke Carburetors. Undoing from four to nine screws enables either the whole top to be lifted off, complete with the float assembly, or else the float bowl, complete with jets, to drop off the bottom. There is a very important gasket between the two halves, and everything must be done to preserve it. A new one can be made from a piece of brown paper, but it is tricky because of all the small holes.

The float will be held with a hinge pin. This is sometimes kept in place with retaining clips, but at other times is free to fall out once the bowl is off the carburetor. Take care not to lose it. When the hinge pin is removed, the float comes off and the needle valve slides out of its housing.

If a float cuts off the supply of fuel too soon, starvation results; if it does not cut it off soon enough excess fuel is allowed into the jets and flooding occurs. In the event of persistent flooding or fuel starvation, the float level needs checking, but as carburetors vary enormously this can only be done by reference to the relevant engine manual.

Two or more jets are screwed into the carburetor at different points. These are small brass fittings with a hole down the center and a screwdriver slot in the top. These and all other drillings and passages must be blown out to make sure there is nothing plugging them up.

Variable-choke Carburetors. The jet can frequently be unscrewed from the base of the carburetor without any other dismantling. If this is the case, count the number of turns taken to unscrew it and put it back the same way. Altering the height of the jet adjusts the fuel mixture.

Variable-choke carburetors have a needle inserted in a piston in the body of the carburetor. The needle drops into the jet. With the air filter off, slip a screwdriver under the edge of this piston, lift it gently, and allow it to fall. It should make a distinct "clunk." If it does not, the piston may be sticking. Remove the chamber from the top of the carburetor and free up the piston at any obvious point of binding.

If the piston is removed from a variable-choke carburetor, take care not to bend the needle hanging from it. If the needle is removed, it must go back in the exact same position, as this, too, will alter the fuel mixture. When the piston is replaced in the carburetor, the needle must slide easily down into its jet.

Carburetor Adjustments.   Make adjustments to the carburetor only when an engine is warm and after checking the points gap, timing, spark plugs, and so on. Many fixed-choke carburetors have only an external screw adjustment to the throttle linkage. Tightening it speeds up the engine idle, while backing it out slows down the idle. Other carburetors also have one or more screws with little springs going into the body of the carburetor—these adjust the mixture in the various jets.

Idle Speed and Mixture Screw. First set the idle speed (normally to around 700 rpm) by adjusting the throttle stop. Now screw in the slow-speed mixture screw (if fitted, it will be the one closest to the engine) until the engine begins to run erratically and slow down. Very slowly back it out. The engine should speed up, reach a peak, and drop off. This peak is the correct mixture setting. To doublecheck the setting, accelerate the engine. If it hesitates, the mixture is too weak and the screw needs to be backed out a little more. The idle speed may now need resetting.

Compound carburetors frequently have two idle screws. They should be moved in and out equal amounts. If an idle setting has been lost, start by turning the screw(s) all the way in, and then back out 1½ turns.

Never do mixture screws up hard. The steel screws can easily damage the soft brass jets.

High-Speed Mixture Screw. If the carburetor has an externally adjustable high-speed jet, this can only be set with the engine under load and above half throttle. Screw it in until the engine slows, and then back it out for the highest speed, as above. Recheck the slow-speed jet.

Variable-choke Carburetors. Variable-choke carburetors sometimes are adjusted by screwing a nut in and out of the base of the carburetor. With the engine idling, screw the nut in until the engine slows and then back it out for maximum speed. Test the setting by inserting a screwdriver under the piston and lifting it 1/16 inch—the engine should speed up and then return to its idle speed. If it remains speeded up, the mixture is too rich and the adjusting screw needs to go in. If the engine slows down, the mixture is too weak and the screw must come out.

Spark Plugs

Removing HT Leads and Plugs. Anytime more than one HT lead is removed from spark plugs or the distributor, all the leads need to be clearly identified for correct replacement. When removing HT leads, twist them first to break them loose, then pull *gently,* grasping the boot. If the lead is stretched, it is likely to break the conductor within, and a new lead will be needed. Clean the area around the plug to stop dirt from falling in the engine. Allow aluminum heads to cool before removing plugs, or else the threads may seize in the head.

Cleaning. The accompanying drawings give a pretty good idea of what plugs can tell us. If reusing old plugs, first thoroughly clean them with a fine file and sandpaper. Work a piece of folded sandpaper between the plug case and the ceramic electrode housing to clean out this area. The plug gap will need to be reset—in the absence of a manual it is hard to be specific, as gaps vary enormously from engine to engine (anywhere from .020 to .080 inch, or 0.50 to 2.00 mm). If no information is available, try .035 inch (0.88 mm), approximately two thumbnail thicknesses. When setting a gap do not lever against the central electrode—the ceramic insulator is easily cracked.

Testing. Hook the spark plug back up to its HT lead, hold it against the engine block, and crank the engine. A clear blue spark should jump from the electrode tip to the ground

Spark-plug diagnostic reference. (Courtesy Champion Spark Plug Company)

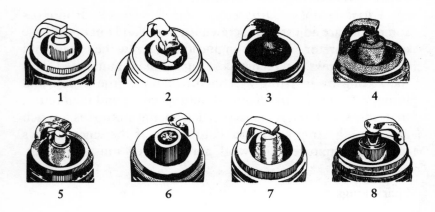

1. Normal. *Core nose lightly coated with grey-brown deposits. Electrodes not burning unduly—gap increasing about .001" per 1,000 miles.*

2. Heavy Deposits. *Possible causes: Fuel or additives; excessive upper cylinder lubricant; worn valve guides; unvarying speed (stationary engine). Plugs should be satisfactory after servicing.*

3. Carbon Fouling. *Deposits can short-circuit the firing end, weakening or eliminating the spark. Check for: Over-rich mixture setting; faulty choke mechanism; clogged air cleaner. Plugs should be satisfactory after servicing.*

4. Oil Fouling. *Deposits can short-circuit the firing end, weakening or eliminating the spark. May be caused by worn valve guides, bores, or piston rings, or by the breaking in of a new or overhauled engine. Cure the oiling problem, if possible. Temporary use of the next hotter grade of plug may stop the misfire. Degrease the plug in solvent before abrasive cleaning. Plugs should be satisfactory after servicing.*

5. Overheating. *Likely causes are: Over-advanced ignition timing; incorrect distributor advance curve; use of fuel with insufficient octane rating; weak mixture. Discard plugs showing signs of overheating, and cure the cause.*

prong. Weak or yellowish sparks indicate an ignition problem (see Ignition Fault Finding above).

Replacement. Before replacing a plug, clean its threads with a wire brush. If the plug body is cut square at the top of its threads, it should have a compression gasket. If not present, the gasket may still be on the cylinder head. It is a common mistake to end up either with two gaskets on one plug or none at all. Either event will detract from engine performance. Plugs cut with a taper at the top of the threads are fitted without a gasket. Gasketed plugs are screwed in hand tight and tightened another quarter turn. Tapered plugs take a one-sixteenth turn. Overtightening may damage a plug and make it extremely hard to get back out.

Operating Problems

Overheating and low oil pressure were covered in Chapter Five, and are treated similarly for gasoline engines. Erratic misfiring on all cylinders is likely to be a fuel problem, while a rhythmic misfiring of one or more cylinders probably is an

---

6. Initial Pre-ignition. *Caused by serious overheating. Causes are those listed for Overheating, but may be more severe. Corrective measures are urgently needed before engine damage occurs. Discard plugs in this condition.*

7. Split Core Nose. *May appear initially as a hairline crack. Probably caused by detonation waves, indicating over-advanced ignition timing; incorrect distributor advance curve; use of fuel with insufficient octane rating; weak mixture; manifold air leaks; cooling system problems; or incorrect gap-setting technique.*

8. Lead Glazing. *Caused by lead additives used in fuel. Deposits can cause misfire. Check carburetion with gas analyzer. Check ignition timing.*

electrical problem. Remove and replace the plug leads one at a time while the engine is running. If the motor slows down when a lead is pulled, it shows that this cylinder is working fine. If no change of note occurs, the cylinder is misfiring. (To be on the safe side, use a rag to grasp the spark plug boots.)

All of the ignition tests in this chapter have been carried out with the engine stopped. When an engine is running the high pressure in the cylinders greatly increases the load on the spark plugs and ignition system. It is possible for everything to check out OK but for the engine still to misfire under load. First check for dirty or improperly gapped plugs. If the plugs look OK, fit new ones (they may be breaking down internally). If only one cylinder is missing, switch its plug for a known good one. If the problem persists, change the HT leads. If the misfiring is

The thermostat housing on an Atomic 4 engine.

accompanied by knocks and a rough idle, the ignition timing may be too far advanced. Overheating and backfiring will occur with retarded ignition. An engine that "bogs down," makes smoke, and shows signs of flooding (gas stains down the carburetor) may simply have a choke stuck in the closed position.

An engine that is running but dies with a lot of knocks and rattles probably has a serious mechanical failure (broken connecting rod, ruined bearing) that cannot be corrected at sea. One that suddenly cuts out most likely has an electrical problem. One that coughs and sputters to a halt has a fuel problem.

7

Troubleshooting Outboard Motors

How They Work

Most outboards are 2-cycle engines (a few are 4-cycle), and all operate in a somewhat different fashion from a diesel or inboard gasoline engine. The key difference is that the crankcase is sealed and the carburetor feeds into the crankcase, and not directly into the engine cylinders. A one-way *reed* or *leaf valve* between the carburetor and crankcase allows the fuel/air mixture to enter the engine but prevents it from blowing back out.

The engine works as follows: As a piston moves up in its cylinder, it compresses the gases in the cylinder and at the same time sucks fuel and air into the crankcase from the carburetor via a leaf valve. Roughly at the top of the piston stroke, a spark ignites the mixture in the cylinder, driving the piston back down. The leaf valve closes and the descending piston pressurizes the fuel/air mixture in the crankcase.

At the bottom of its stroke, the piston uncovers a series of holes (ports) in its cylinder wall. Some lead to the exhaust, some into the crankcase. The exhaust ports are a little higher in the cylinder wall and uncover a fraction before the inlet ports. Most of the exhaust gases exit the cylinder, and then, as the inlet ports uncover, the pressurized fuel/air mixture in the crankcase rushes into the cylinder, pushing the remainder of the burnt gases out of the exhaust. The piston now comes back up, blocks off the ports, and once again compresses the mixture in the cylinder at the same time that it sucks a fresh charge into the crankcase.

If an engine has more than one cylinder, each section of the crankcase is sealed from the next so that all the pistons operate as individual crankcase pumps. Two-cycle engines are more sensitive to "blow-by" and loss of compression than four-cycle inboard gasoline engines. When a piston is on its compression stroke, if the mixture is blowing down the sides of the piston into the crankcase, no vacuum will develop in the crankcase, no fuel mixture will be sucked in, and the engine will not run.

Carburetion

With the exception of the leaf-valve assembly, carburetion is just the same as on inboard gasoline engines. Multicylinder outboards frequently have two or more carburetors. Motors

Principles of 2-cycle outboard operation. (1) The piston moves up, compressing the mixture in the cylinder and sucking fuel and air into the crankcase. The reed (leaf) valve is open. (2) Ignition: The piston moves back down, the reed valve closes, and the mixture in the crankcase is compressed. (3) The piston uncovers the exhaust and inlet ports at the bottom of its stroke. The compressed mixture in the crankcase rushes into the cylinder, driving out the exhaust.

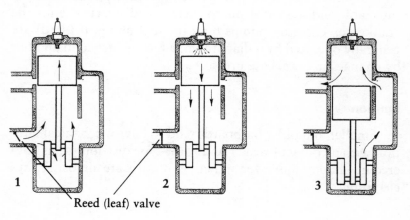

Reed (leaf) valve

with more than one carburetor have no externally adjustable jet mixture screws. Instead, the carburetors are balanced by altering the throttle linkages in order to run the motor as fast and smoothly as possible for any given throttle setting.

Lubrication

Outboard engines have no valves in their cylinders and no oil sump. Lubrication is achieved by mixing oil with the gas. When the mixture is drawn into the crankcase a fine mist of oil is distributed all around the moving parts. On most outboards the oil is mixed with the gas in the fuel tank, using mixtures of anywhere from 25 parts gas to 1 part oil (25:1) to 50:1. Only proper outboard motor oil should be used. Other engine oils contain additives that may harm the motor.

Outboard motor fuel has a tendency to sit around for long periods of time in half-filled tanks. Water (from condensation) and dirt gather in the tank, lacquer from the oil coats the fuel system, and starting and operating difficulties are the result. Therefore, old fuel should be dumped at regular intervals by turning the tank upside down (draining through the fuel line will leave the dirt and water in the tank), but *please* don't dump the fuel on the ground or the water. Take it to an automotive service center; they'll combine it with used motor oil in their waste-redemption tank, and eventually it will be re-refined and recycled.

On larger and newer outboards, the oil is put into a separate tank and a special pump meters and injects it into the crankcase. These oil pumps (and the fuel pump, if fitted) are generally operated by a diaphragm, which is sucked in and out by changes in crankcase pressure.

Ignition

Smaller and older outboards tend to have mechanical ignition with a contact breaker and rotor-type distributor, as covered in Chapter 6. Newer and larger models are almost always electronic.

Electronic ignition on a Mercury outboard. About all that can be done with it is to clean the terminals and spray everything with WD 40.

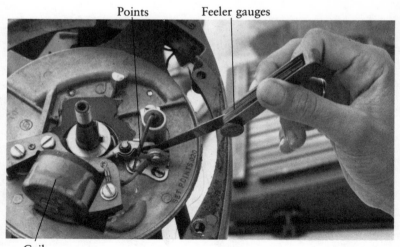

Points   Feeler gauges

Coil

Checking the points gap on a Johnson outboard with mechanical ignition. (Note: the flywheel has been removed.)

Failure to Start

Some outboards with electric starts have a "neutral start" switch that prevents the motor from being cranked in gear. If it won't crank, check the gear shift. If it still won't crank, refer to the Failure to Crank section in Chapter 5.

If the motor cranks but refuses to fire, pull an HT lead from a spark plug, hold it ¼ inch from a good ground (a clean section of the engine block away from the carburetor), and crank the engine. No spark indicates an ignition problem. A spark means there is probably a carburetion problem, fouled plugs, or both. Remove a plug and check it before assuming carburetor troubles.

Ignition Fault Finding

Replace the HT lead on the spark plug and pull its other end out of the coil. Hold it off its socket and crank again. A spark tells us we have a defective HT lead to the plug. (It may only be dirty or wet, and "tracking" to ground.) If there is no spark and we have electronic ignition, we are out of luck. The

An easily constructed test light with its own power source. The bulb should light when wire clamps are touching.

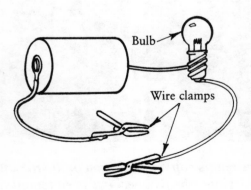

best that can be done is to clean all the leads and terminals, spray everything liberally with WD 40, and try again. If the unit has a contact breaker and distributor, check it out as outlined in the section on Ignition Fault Finding in Chapter 6. Note: On outboards without electric starting, there is no voltage in the system to carry out tests using a test lamp when the motor is stopped. A test lamp will have to be made up with its own power source as illustrated.

Flywheel Removal. It is nearly always necessary to remove the flywheel to gain access to the contact breaker. A special puller is called for, but is not necessary if this procedure is followed:

1. Remove the flywheel cover with recoil starter (if fitted).
2. Undo the central nut holding the flywheel until the nut is *flush with the top of the threads on the shaft.*
3. Have someone hold the motor up with their hands *under the flywheel,* supporting the weight of the motor with the flywheel.
4. Place a solid block of wood on the nut and hit it smartly to jar the flywheel loose.
5. Remove the nut the rest of the way and lift off the flywheel, taking care not to lose its key.

Carburetion Fault Finding

Pull the spark plug(s) and inspect them. A wet plug indicates flooding. Open the choke, place the throttle in the wide-open position, give the gas a minute or two to evaporate, and crank the engine again. Persistent flooding will require taking the carburetor apart, checking the float for a hole or saturation, checking the float level, and inspecting the float chamber needle valve. (All steps are covered in Chapter 6.)

Dry plugs can result from either fuel starvation or a failure of the crankcase seal. Has the throttle been placed in the "start" position? Is there fuel in the tank? If so, then break the fuel line loose at the carburetor and check the flow.

There are two types of fuel supply:

1. Gravity Feed. The fuel tank is mounted on top of the motor with a filter inside the tank (on the fuel outlet) and a filter screen where the fuel line goes into the carburetor. Fuel should flow freely when the fuel line is disconnected from the carburetor.

2. Separate tanks. These have a hand bulb to pump up the fuel supply for starting, and are always accompanied by a separate, engine-operated diaphragm fuel pump. To check the fuel supply, first disconnect the fitting on the fuel line that plugs into the motor. Direct the hose into a can, depress the ball in the check valve with a nail (or something similar), and squeeze the bulb on the fuel line. Gas should flow freely. Take care not to damage the O-ring seal inside the valve or else air will be sucked into the engine when it is running, causing surging and stalling.

   If fuel is not flowing, check the line and bulb for cracked or perished rubber. If the line is OK, remove the filter from the tank and clean it. This is done by backing out the four screws that hold the exit fitting to the top of the tank. Take this opportunity to blow through the fuel line and clear it of any obstructions before replacing the filter. The hand bulb should now produce a good flow.

   Reconnect the fuel line to the motor. If fuel starvation still seems to be a problem, disconnect the fuel line at the carburetor and crank the engine 10 or 12 times—the fuel

Externally adjustable jets on a Johnson outboard.

High-speed jet mixture screw   Idle mixture screw

Fixed-choke carburetor with float bowl removed.

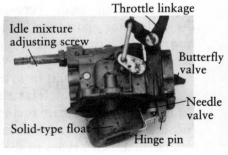

Throttle linkage

Idle mixture adjusting screw

Butterfly valve

Needle valve

Solid-type float

Hinge pin

TROUBLESHOOTING OUTBOARD MOTOR CARBURETION: QUICK REFERENCE

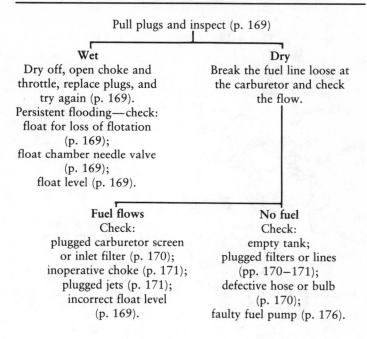

Pull plugs and inspect (p. 169)

Wet
Dry off, open choke and
throttle, replace plugs, and
try again (p. 169).
Persistent flooding—check:
float for loss of flotation
(p. 169);
float chamber needle valve
(p. 169);
float level (p. 169).

Dry
Break the fuel line loose at
the carburetor and check
the flow.

Fuel flows
Check:
plugged carburetor screen
or inlet filter (p. 170);
inoperative choke (p. 171);
plugged jets (p. 171);
incorrect float level
(p. 169).

No fuel
Check:
empty tank;
plugged filters or lines
(pp. 170–171);
defective hose or bulb
(p. 170);
faulty fuel pump (p. 176).

pump should also produce a steady flow. If it does, check the inlet screen on the carburetor, or the carburetor-mounted fuel filter (if fitted). Depending on the engine, there may or may not be another fuel filter fitted before the fuel pump. If there is, it too must be cleaned.

If the filters are OK and the fuel pump is working, then the choke and carburetor jets need inspecting (see below). If the fuel pump does not produce a steady flow, see the section on fuel pumps.

Chokes and Jets.   Maybe the choke isn't working. Some are manually operated flaps. These are foolproof. Others are manually or electrically operated "primers," piston devices similar to an accelerator pump that squirt an extra shot of fuel

TWO SIMPLE FIXED-CHOKE CARBURETORS

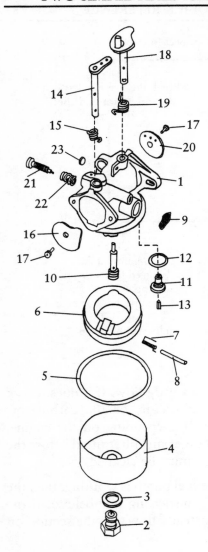

1. Carburetor body
2. Jet retainer screw
3. Jet retainer gasket
4. Fuel bowl
5. Fuel bowl gasket
6. Float
7. Float spring
8. Hinge pin
9. Fuel inlet screen
10. Nozzle
11. Inlet seat
12. Inlet needle gasket
13. Inlet needle
14. Choke shaft
15. Choke return spring
16. Choke plate
17. Choke plate screw
18. Throttle shaft
19. Throttle return spring
20. Throttle shutter
21. Idle mixture screw
22. Idle mixture screw spring
23. Welch plug

Center-bowl carburetor. (Courtesy Mercury Outboards)

into the engine. Crank the engine and operate the device repeatedly, and then check the plugs. They should be wet. If not, choke the engine by setting the throttle wide open, more or less blocking the air inlet (on the carburetor) with a hand, and cranking. (To get at the carburetor on many outboards, you'll

Exploded view of the carburetor used on OMC's 1½ hp models. Do not attempt to clean float in solvent. (Courtesy OMC)

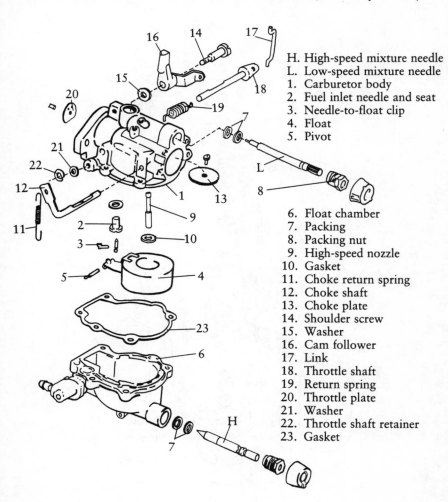

H. High-speed mixture needle
L. Low-speed mixture needle
1. Carburetor body
2. Fuel inlet needle and seat
3. Needle-to-float clip
4. Float
5. Pivot

6. Float chamber
7. Packing
8. Packing nut
9. High-speed nozzle
10. Gasket
11. Choke return spring
12. Choke shaft
13. Choke plate
14. Shoulder screw
15. Washer
16. Cam follower
17. Link
18. Throttle shaft
19. Return spring
20. Throttle plate
21. Washer
22. Throttle shaft retainer
23. Gasket

have to remove the engine cowling.) If the engine fires, progressively unblock the air inlet to maintain a partial choke while things warm up.

If fuel starvation is a result of blocked jets, dismantle and clean the carburetor, as detailed in Chapter 6.

A simple variable-choke carburetor. (Courtesy British Seagull)

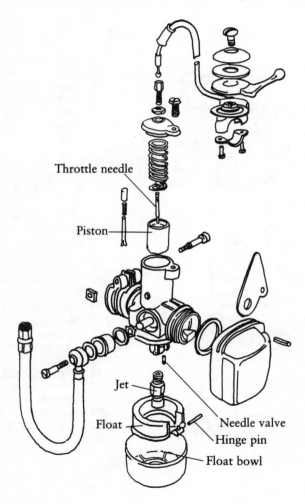

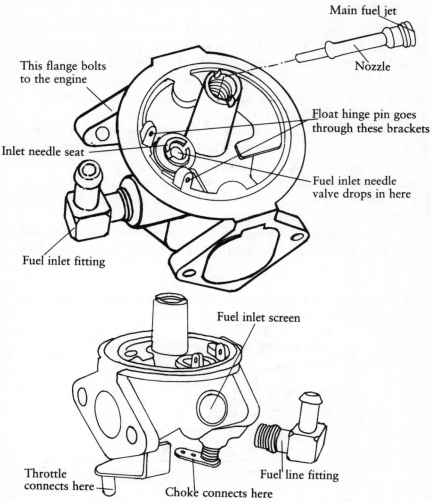

Main fuel jet

Nozzle

This flange bolts
to the engine

Float hinge pin goes
through these brackets

Inlet needle seat

Fuel inlet needle
valve drops in here

Fuel inlet fitting

Fuel inlet screen

Throttle
connects here

Fuel line fitting

Choke connects here

*Location of fuel inlet screen, fuel inlet needle valve, and main
jet assembly on a Mercury center-bowl carburetor. The carburetor body is upside down in both these illustrations, with the
bowl, float, and fuel inlet needle valve removed. (Courtesy
Clymer Publications)*

Fuel Pumps

Some fuel pumps are mounted on the crankcase, with a drilled hole in the crankcase transmitting pressure changes to a diaphragm. Others are mounted elsewhere on the engine or on the side of the carburetor, with a hose leading from the crankcase to the pump diaphragm. All can be found by tracing the fuel line from the fuel tank to the carburetor.

A pinhole in a diaphragm will generally not prevent fuel pump or engine operation. What is more likely is that at idle speeds gas entering the crankcase through the pinhole will wet the plug and produce symptoms of flooding. At higher speeds, the small amount of fuel involved will not have a noticeable effect on engine performance.

More severe diaphragm failure or trash in the valves will make the fuel pump inoperative. The valves can be tested by

Outboard motor fuel pump. This pump is shown using leaf (reed) valves. Others use spring-loaded ball valves.

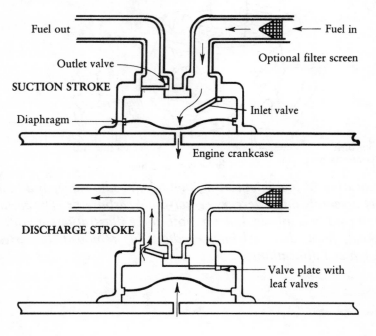

sucking and blowing on the inlet and outlet ports on the pump. It should be possible to blow through the inlet side, but not suck, and to suck through the outlet side, but not blow. Removing the pump cover provides access to the valves and diaphragm. Some pumps use leaf valves, others, spring-loaded ball valves. With the latter, when the pump cover is removed watch out for springs and balls!

Failed valves can be overridden by pumping gently and continuously on the hand bulb, or else by removing the valves and setting the fuel tank above the engine for a gravity feed. In the case of a seriously damaged diaphragm the fuel line can be disconnected from the pump, connected directly to the carburetor, and the same two methods used to maintain fuel flow. The pump inlet and outlet ports will need plugging to prevent the crankcase ventilating to atmosphere through the broken diaphragm.

Crankcase Compression and Cold Starting

As previously noted, any leaks in the crankcase seals will seriously affect performance and starting. There are three possible problem areas: blow-by past the piston rings, leaking leaf valves in the intake manifold, or leaking crankcase seals at the gasket and crankshaft. Sometimes the metal of a crankcase itself becomes porous.

Blow-By. Blow-by is especially likely when the engine is cold or after long periods of shut-down when the film of lubricating oil on the cylinder walls drains off. Squirting some oil into the cylinders through the plug holes should solve the problem, but no more than a couple of shots should be put in each cylinder or piston damage may result. Heating spark plugs with, say, a cigarette lighter will help with difficult starting, but be sure there are no gasoline vapors around!

Leaf (Reed) Valves. Leaf valves consist of thin plates of spring steel fastened on one edge to a machined base plate, with an opening under each leaf. When a piston ascends its cylinder, it sucks the leaf off its base and draws in fuel and air. When the piston descends its cylinder, it pushes the leaf against its base plate, thus sealing the crankcase.

Leaf valves can only be checked by removing the carburetor. There is in any case little that can be done with them at sea. If leaf valves are bent, corroded, chipped, cracked, or distorted in any way, they need replacing. It may be possible to temporarily improve their seating in some instances by taking them apart and cleaning them and the base plate. Though it may be tempting to refit them in reverse so they will seal better, don't try it. They are liable to break off in use and do serious damage to the engine.

Leaking crankcase seals are beyond the scope of this book; fortunately this is an unlikely cause of sudden engine failure.

Operating Problems

One way to avoid problems with an outboard is always to stand it up and drain out all water before laying it down for inspection or work. If this is not done, cooling water is liable to find its way into the engine via the exhaust ports and do expen-

Leaf (reed) valve assembly, viewed from the side of the engine.

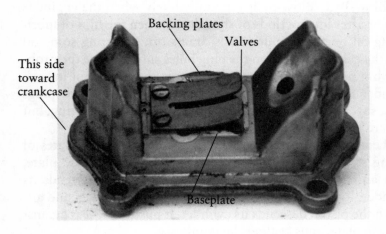

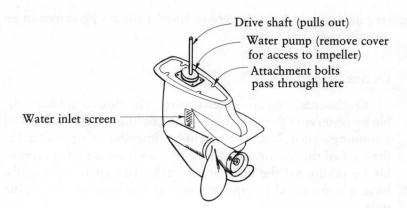

Drive shaft (pulls out)

Water pump (remove cover for access to impeller)

Attachment bolts pass through here

Water inlet screen

Typical lower end.

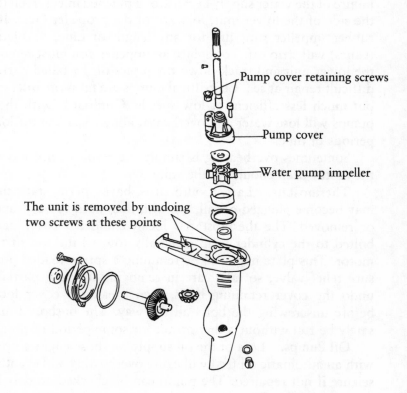

Pump cover retaining screws

Pump cover

Water pump impeller

The unit is removed by undoing two screws at these points

The lower unit on an OMC outboard. (Courtesy OMC)

sive damage. Also, an outboard should *always* be stored in an upright position.

Overheating

Outboards are raw-water cooled. The flow is readily visible by observing the stream of water coming out of the back of a running motor. Normally, a rubber impeller pump is fitted in the base of the motor, just above the lower unit, and is accessible by taking off the unit. Some outboards, such as Seagulls, have a centrifugal pump mounted in the base of the engine unit.

Water Pumps.   Overheating is almost always due to a failure of the water supply because of a plugged inlet screen (on the side of the lower unit, forward of the propeller face). If a rubber impeller runs dry for any length of time, its blades (vanes) will strip off. To replace an impeller you must remove the lower unit and track down the pieces of the failed part, a difficult repair at sea. Centrifugal pumps are far more tolerant, but much less efficient at low speeds. Outboards with these pumps will lose water and overheat if allowed to idle for long periods of time.

Sometimes overheating is simply the result of not having the motor deep enough in the water.

Thermostats.   Larger outboards have thermostats that may become plugged or fail, and will then need to be cleaned or removed. The thermostat is located under a cover plate bolted to the cylinder head, generally toward the top of the motor. This plate may also be retaining a spring-loaded pressure relief valve, so take care in removing it. First, partially undo the cover retaining bolts, then break the cover loose before unscrewing the bolts all the way. The outboard may safely be run without a thermostat for some period of time.

Oil Pumps.   Loss of the oil supply on those engines fitted with an automatic oil feed will cause overheating and eventual seizure if not repaired. The pump can be checked crudely by unscrewing the fitting where the discharge hose (the *pulse hose*) goes into the crankcase. The end of this fitting, which contains a flame arrestor, may be plugged with carbon. If the hole in the crankcase is temporarily blocked, and the engine idled, oil should "pulse" out of this fitting. This should not be done for more than a few seconds! If the pump is not working, check its "pick-up" (supply) hose for clogging.

Oil pumps are not repairable at sea. Carry a spare can of outboard motor oil and add it to the fuel tank in the proportion of 50:1 if an oil pump failure is suspected. Even if the pump is actually working, the excess oil will do no harm beyond causing the engine to smoke and the plugs to foul over time.

Misfiring and Backfiring

Check for dirty fuel or a low gas tank. If the vent screw or hole in the gas tank filler cap is plugged up, a vacuum will form in the tank and the engine will be starved of fuel. The spark plug leads should be pulled by turns to determine if all cylinders are misfiring or just one or two. (See the Operating Problems section of Chapter 6.) If the former, it is probably a fuel problem. In the latter case, look for an ignition problem. All the HT leads need to be checked for loose terminals, damaged insulation, or moisture. A good shot of WD 40 may clear things up.

Misfiring only under a heavy load (for example, when accelerating) is normally caused by a faulty spark plug. But if the engine momentarily dies and then picks up when the throttle is first opened, dirty fuel or jets is more likely.

Aside from the ignition and carburetion problems already discussed, sometimes a flywheel will work loose on its key (the piece of metal that locks it to its shaft) and will begin to slip. Ignition timing is determined by the position of the flywheel in relation to the crankshaft, so this will throw out the timing. If the key is still usable, realigning the flywheel with the keyway and tightening the flywheel retaining nut should get you home. If the key has been stripped, short of finding a piece of metal to replace the key temporarily, there is little that can be done. Finally, if the engine is backfiring through the carburetor, it may have a broken leaf valve, which cannot be repaired at sea.

Loss of Drive

On larger outboards, the propeller is mounted to its boss (center unit) on a rubber shock-absorbing pad. If the propeller strikes a solid object the rubber tears up, thus protecting the rest of the engine from damage.

On smaller outboards, the same function is served by a *shear pin* or by mounting the propeller on a spring (as in the Seagull motors).

A shear pin can be replaced in an emergency with any suitably sized piece of metal, although one or two spares

A typical shear pin configuration.

should *always* be carried on board. A spring can be bent back into shape. A rubber hub, however, cannot be jury rigged; carry a spare propeller unit for this type of motor. If none is aboard, the hub will generally impart enough drive to the propeller to keep moving at idle speeds.

Failure to Start when Hot

Sometimes when the motor is shut down, the heat of the engine will cause gas in the carburetor float bowl to vaporize. This pressurizes the bowl, and depending on the location of the

The pin is not a shear pin—it merely holds the assembly together. The sturdy spring substitutes for a shear pin.

Spring

idle jet, may push gas into the engine inlet manifold. Any attempt to restart the motor results in flooding. The solution is to close the fuel valve, open the choke and throttle wide, wait a minute, and crank until the excess fuel is cleared.

Submersion

"Submersion is about the worst thing that can happen to an engine . . . . this is why we always recommend owners to *secure it with a safety lanyard . . . .*" (From a Seagull engine manual.) Wise words indeed! Saltwater submersion is especially damaging to engines.

Following a dunking, the engine must be *immediately* washed down and flushed out in fresh water—certainly within

A rubber hub replaces the shear pin on this unit.

three hours. The exterior should be thoroughly hosed down; all HT leads and electrical connections should be broken loose and washed, paying particular attention to terminal sockets; and the carburetor and fuel system should be dismantled and flushed with clean water. On some engines, it may be necessary to remove the flywheel to rinse off the electrical components properly.

Remove the spark plugs, place the engine with the plug holes down, and turn it over until all water is expelled. Two-stroke oil should be placed in the engine inlet manifold and spark plug hole(s) and the engine spun a few times.

Dry off, reassemble, and *start* the engine as soon as possible, except as noted below. The electrical system should be given a good spraying of WD 40, if available. If the motor won't start, pull the plugs and check for water. If any is present, dry them off and try again.

When the engine fires up, it should be given a good long run. Double the oil ratio in the fuel mixture for a few hours for extra lubrication. If the motor went down in salt water, it should be completely disassembled and cleaned at the first opportunity. Tiny specks of salt lodged in the engine can destroy polished metal surfaces and electrical connections.

If the engine filled with sandy or silted water, do *not* start it until it is thoroughly cleaned. Scoring of the pistons, cylinders, and bearings will rapidly destroy it. Likewise, if it was running when it sank, it may have bent connecting rods. If there is any binding when it is turned over, do not start it. If the motor cannot be started, and it will be some time before it can be attended to, the best thing is to store it in a tank of fresh water to keep the air out of it and slow corrosion to a minimum.

8

Towing and Abandoning Ship

If all your efforts fail to get your vessel moving again, or water is coming in faster than you can pump it out, and there is no safe haven within reach, it may be time to think about getting rescued.

First of all, it is necessary to get your rescuer's attention.

Distress Signals

Do not use distress signals unless in distress! Not only can the abuse of distress signals lay you open to a salvage claim and expensive legal costs (see Salvages, below) but it is also one of the reasons why the government keeps thinking of imposing costly Coast Guard user fees on the boating public.

When close inshore or within sight of another vessel, try the VHF radio first. The internationally monitored VHF channel for distress calls is channel 16. (On single sideband frequencies, it is 2182 kHz.) VHF is "line of sight" only. It will not work at a range of much over 30 miles in the best circumstances and may be limited to only a few hundred yards if there is a hill or any other obstruction between the sender and receiver.

Other distress signals, *which are only of use if a potential rescuer is in sight,* are:

- Daytime—Orange smoke bombs or dye in the water; in sunlight use a mirror to beam the sun at passing vessels; wave your hands or boat cushions slowly from side to side above your head.
- Nighttime—Orange flares or parachute flares. White parachute flares, spotlights, and strobe lights are very effective in attracting attention, though not recognized distress signals.

My own experience and that of many others confirms that even at close quarters and in busy shipping lanes distress signals are frequently just not seen by passing ships. It is difficult to have too many flares on board. The best ones are red rocket and parachute flares.

Flares should always be let off in pairs a few seconds apart. The first one may only vaguely catch someone's attention. This person will then be looking around more alertly. The second flare will confirm that there is an emergency on hand. Without it the watcher may conclude that the first was just a trick of the imagination. Once a rescuer's attention has been gained it is important to maintain a steady light for them to steer toward, since your boat, dinghy, or liferaft will be bobbing in and out of sight.

Flares have a limited shelf life, with an expiration date stamped on the side. You should keep them current (as they must be to meet Coast Guard regulations). One or two of the older ones can be used to gain experience in letting them off—taking care not to start a rescue procedure, of course.

An EPIRB is for use offshore when no potential rescuers are in the vicinity. EPIRBs, when turned on, automatically transmit a distress signal on which rescuers can home. They come in three "classes"—A, B, and C. Type C transmit on VHF, over short distances, and are only suitable for coastal cruising. Even then there seems little chance of a class C signal being picked up and recognized—their usefulness is very much in question.

Type A and B EPIRBs both transmit on 121.5 MHz and 243 MHz over a range of up to 300 miles and for a period of up to 10 days. All major aircraft and many satellites monitor these frequencies. If any signal is picked up it is reported to the relevant authorities and a search initiated. The only difference between A and B EPIRBs is that the former are activated automatically, while the latter have to be turned on by hand.

Satellite coverage of A and B EPIRBs is excellent in the Northern Hemisphere, but there are large areas of the Southern Hemisphere where, due to a lack of satellite tracking stations, a signal is likely to go undetected. These areas are also the least frequented by commercial aircraft, further reducing the chances of rescue. Steps are under way to rectify this with a new worldwide frequency of 406 MHz, but it will be some time before this is fully operational, and the new EPIRBs are likely to be much more expensive.

The flare kit and EPIRB should always be kept in a protected but easily accessible location. In the event of a rapid evacuation of the boat in the dark there will be no time or light to go digging around in lockers looking for them.

Towing

In any kind of sea there is great danger in having a towboat, especially a large one, come alongside to take a line. Far better to buoy the end of a line with boat cushions or fenders, trail it downwind, and let the towboat pick it up with a boathook.

Unless the conditions are calm, towing will impose great strains on your boat. A towing bridle should be made up and fastened to a number of strong points on the boat to spread the load. Good candidates are mooring cleats, winches, the samson post, and the mast, but note that a line attached directly to a deck-stepped mast may pull it off its heel fitting and bring it down. *Under no circumstances should any crew stand within the bight of the line.*

Regardless of where the towline is attached, *it must lead through a towpoint at the stemhead* in order to keep the boat head into the seas. Should the pull come from any other point farther aft, the boat will start sheering wildly from side to side and may well roll itself under.

A sailboat has a limited maximum speed—its "hull speed." In all likelihood a towing boat may move at higher speeds. If any sailboat is towed at much above its hull speed, *enormous loads are imposed upon it that can end up doing extensive damage.* Be sure to agree on a safe towing speed before the tow commences. In many instances large ships cannot maneuver at slow enough speeds to pull a small sailboat in safety—it will be better to forego the tow.

Before commencing the tow, if there will be no radio contact, agree on a series of hand signals for essential maneuvers (for example, slow down; speed up; turn to port; turn to starboard; cut me loose).

A nylon rope used as a towline will stretch and provide something of a shock absorber, but should it break it will whip back with dangerous force. Braided nylon has less whip while still providing some elasticity, and is therefore to be preferred over 3-strand.

The towline should be adjusted so that the towed boat is one or more wave crests behind the towing boat. This will reduce any tendency to surf up the back in following seas, and cut down on shock loads in head seas.

An ax or large serrated knife should be kept handy in case it is necessary to cut loose in a hurry (but not under a load).

Salvage

Salvage is a very complicated business covered by its own body of law. In general, a towing or salvaging boat is entitled to fair compensation, and if your boat would otherwise have been lost, this may amount to full salvage rights.

• If you attract another boat's attention by the use of distress signals you strengthen any salvage claim.

• If you accept a tow using another boat's towline you may strengthen any salvage claim.
• If you agree on a towing fee in the presence of witnesses, even if only verbally, before accepting a tow, this supersedes salvage rights in any legal arguments.

Abandoning Ship

If, in spite of all efforts, the water level in a boat is rising uncontrollably, it is essential to detail crewmembers to make preparations for abandoning ship. All the crew should long ago have put on life jackets and safety harnesses. The liferaft will need to be inflated or the dinghy readied, and the following items put aboard: water, food, rudimentary navigation equipment (if necessary), an EPIRB (which should already be switched on), flares, a flashlight, line, knives (properly sheathed so as not to puncture the raft), a medical kit with seasickness pills, something to bail with, paddles, bellows and a repair kit for a rubber raft, a can opener, a fishing kit, and above all *plenty of clothing* since exposure is likely to be the greatest problem encountered. Foil-backed plastic "space blankets" are excellent for conserving body heat. Water is best placed in plastic containers that are not quite full—they will float if thrown overboard.

Unless lives are in immediate danger, the boat should not be abandoned until it sinks. This was one of the primary lessons of the 1979 Fastnet tragedy, in which a number of crews took to their liferafts. Several of the waterlogged boats survived the storm, while some of those on the liferafts perished. It is essential, however, to keep a good knife on a lanyard around your neck so as to be able to cut the painter or lifelines in a hurry if the sinking boat threatens to pull the raft or any crewmembers under.

In general, even if you abandon your boat, as long as it remains afloat it will be more visible than a liferaft, and it is better to stay close to it.

Boarding Rescue Ships

Coming alongside a rescue ship is a highly dangerous proposition. At slow speeds the ship's captain will have no maneuverability. The overhanging bow and stern will probably bring down your boat's rigging. The boat itself will be crashing up and down against the side of the ship with each passing wave, easily by as much as ten to twenty feet. *Boarding ships in rough seas from a small boat should only be done as a last resort if lives are in immediate danger.* Far better to wait for proper rescue services or board a small fishing vessel if one is in the vicinity. If this is not possible, it is preferable to have the ship's captain launch a lifeboat and pick you and your crew up. If a ship has to be boarded directly, everything possible must be done to keep it to windward, allowing it to drift down slowly on your sailboat, providing partial protection in its lee.

Long before the two boats are close enough to jump for dangling ladders, nets, or ropes, you should be watching the rolling of the ship, gauging the waves, and estimating the point at which your boat is going to be highest in relation to the ship. This is the moment to grab a rope or ladder and start climbing, straining every nerve and muscle fiber in your body to get clear of your boat and its rigging. You should attempt to leave your boat well forward or aft to clear the masts and spreaders. In all cases of rescue at sea, safety harnesses as well as life jackets should be worn. The rescuers may be able to clip a line to the harness and pull or winch a crewmember to safety.

Rescue by Helicopter

Rescue by helicopter cannot be done from the deck of a sailboat—the risk of entangling the helicopter's hoisting cable in the mast and rigging is too great. It may be possible to put the whole crew in a dinghy or liferaft and stream this downwind of the boat on a long line to give the helicopter sufficient clearance from your boat. At night, carry a flashlight in the liferaft to illuminate it for the pilot. Rescue can then be effected directly from the liferaft.

Static electricity can build up on hoisting cables and baskets. To avoid shock allow them to ground out on the liferaft or water before grabbing them. If there is any kind of a sea running, the liferaft will be bobbing up and down and the basket shooting in and out of reach. Good timing and strong arms will be needed to get aboard. Weaker crewmembers must be helped up first.

If it is not possible to be rescued directly from the liferaft when the rescue cable is lowered, probably with a rescuer on it, the boat's crew will have to take to the water one at a time in life jackets to be winched up.

For obvious reasons, *no line from a helicopter should ever be made fast to your boat!*

Freeing Frozen Parts and Fasteners

Problems with frozen fasteners are inevitable on boats. One or more of the following techniques may free things up.

Lubrication

• Clean everything with a wire brush (preferably one with brass bristles), douse liberally with penetrating oil, and wait. Find something else to do for an hour or two, overnight if possible, before having another go. Be patient.
• Clevis pins: After lubricating and waiting, grip the large end of the pin with Vise-Grips (mole wrench) and turn the pin in its socket to free it. If the pin is the type with a cotter pin (also known as a cotter key or split pin) in both ends, remove one of the cotter pins, grip the clevis pin, and turn. Since the Vise-Grips will probably mar the surface of the pin, it should be knocked out from the other end.

Shock Treatment

An impact wrench is a handy tool to have around. These take a variety of end fittings (screwdriver bits; sockets) to match different fasteners. The wrench is hit hard with a hammer and hopefully jars the fastener loose. If an impact wrench is not available or does not work, other forms of shock must be applied with an acute sense of the breaking point of the fastener and adjacent engine castings, etc. Unfortunately this is generally only acquired after a lifetime of breaking things! Depending on the problem, shock treatment may take different forms:

• A bolt stuck in an engine block: Put a sizable punch squarely on the head of the bolt and give it a good knock into the block. Now try undoing it.

- A pulley on a tapered shaft, a propeller, or an outboard motor flywheel: Back out the retaining nut *until its face is flush with the end of the shaft* (this is important to avoid damage to the threads on the nut or shaft). Put pressure behind the pulley, propeller, or flywheel as if trying to pull it off, and hit the end of the retaining nut or shaft smartly. The shock will frequently break things loose without the need for a specialized puller.
- A large nut with limited room around it, or one on a shaft that wants to turn (for example, a crankshaft pulley nut): Put a short-handled wrench on the nut, hold the wrench to prevent it from jumping off, and hit it hard.
- If all else fails, use a cold chisel to cut a slot in the side of the offending nut or the head of the bolt, place a punch in the slot at a tangential angle to the nut or bolt, and hit it smartly.

Leverage

- Screws: With a square-bladed screwdriver, put a crescent (adjustable) wrench on the blade, bear down hard on the screw, and turn the screwdriver with the wrench. If the screwdriver has a round blade, clamp a pair of Vise-Grips to the base of the handle and do the same thing.
- Nuts and bolts: If using wrenches with one box end and one open end, put the box end of the appropriate wrench on the fastener and hook the box end of the next size up into the free open end of the wrench to double the length of the handle and thus the leverage.
- Cheater pipe: Slip a length of pipe over the handle of the wrench to increase its leverage.

Heat

Heat expands metal, but for this treatment to be effective, frozen fasteners must frequently be raised to cherry-red temperatures. These temperatures will upset tempering in hardened steel, while uneven heating of surrounding castings may cause them to crack. Heat must be applied with circumspection.

Heat applied to a frozen nut will expand it outward, and it can then be broken loose. But equally, heat applied to the bolt will expand it within the nut, generating all kinds of pressure that helps to break the grip of rust, etc. When the fixture cools it will frequently come apart quite easily.

Broken Fasteners

- Rounded-off heads: Sometimes there is not enough head left on a fastener to grip with Vise-Grips or pipe (Stillson) wrenches, but there is enough to accept a slot made by a hacksaw. A screwdriver can then be inserted and turned as above.
- If a head breaks off it is often possible to remove whatever it was holding, thus exposing part of the shaft of the fastener, which can be lubricated, gripped with Vise-Grips, and backed out.
- Drilling out: It is very important to drill down the center of a broken fastener. Use a center punch and take some time putting an accurate "dimple" at this point before attempting to drill. Next use a small drill to make a pilot hole to the desired depth. If Ezy-Outs or "screw extractors" (hardened, tapered steel screws with reversed threads, available from tool supply houses) are on hand, drill the correctly sized hole for the appropriate Ezy-Out and try extracting the stud. Otherwise drill out the stud *up to the insides of its threads but no farther,* or irrepairable damage will be done to the threads in the casting. The remaining bits of fastener thread in the casting can be picked out with judicious use of a small screwdriver or some pointed instrument. If a tap is available to clean up the threads, so much the better.
- Pipe fittings: If a hacksaw blade can be gotten inside the relevant fittings (which can often be done using duct tape to make a handle on the blade), cut a slit in the fitting along its length, and then place a punch on the outside alongside

the cut, hit it, and collapse it inward. Do the same on the other side of the cut. The fitting should now come out easily.

Miscellaneous

• Stainless steel: Stainless-to-stainless fasteners (for example, many turnbuckles) have a bad habit of "galling" when being done up or undone, especially if there is any dirt in the threads to cause friction. Galling (otherwise known as "cold welding") is a process in which molecules on the surface of one part of the fastener transfer to the other part. Everything seizes up for good. Galled stainless fastenings cannot be salvaged—they almost always end up shearing off. When doing up or undoing a stainless fastener, if any sudden or unusual friction develops stop immediately, let it cool off, lubricate thoroughly, work the fastener backward and forward to spread the lubrication around, go back the other way, clean the threads, and start again.

• Aluminum: Aluminum oxidizes to form a dense white powder. Aluminum oxide is more voluminous than the original aluminum and so generates a lot of pressure around any fasteners passing through aluminum fixtures—sometimes enough pressure to shear off the heads of fasteners. Once oxidation around a stainless or bronze fastener has reached a certain point it is virtually impossible to remove the fastener without breaking it.

• Damaged threads: If all else fails, and a fastener has to be drilled out, the threads in the casting may be damaged. There are two options.

  1. To drill and tap for the next larger fastener.
  2. To install a Heli-Coil insert. A Heli-Coil is a new thread. An oversized hole is drilled and tapped with a special tap, and the Heli-Coil insert (the new thread) is screwed into the hole with a special tool. You end up with the original sized hole and threads. Any good machine shop will have the relevant tools and inserts.

Tools and Spares

The following is a suggested list of tools and spares for some moderately serious cruising. It is a good idea to organize tools according to categories (for example, woodworking; mechanics; electrical) although I never seem to be able to do a job without having to turn out every locker on the boat! Many people like plastic fishing tackle boxes for storing their tools. Personally I prefer large Tupperware (or similar) containers. These are not as convenient as tackle boxes but are completely airtight: if tools are cleaned and given a shot of WD 40 before going in they will last indefinitely without rusting. Engine parts (such as injectors) can be further protected by first soaking in diesel and then storing in Zip Loc bags.

Mechanic's tools

Open end/box end wrench set, 3/8" to 3/4"
3/8" drive socket set, 3/8" to 3/4"
(Substitute metric wrenches and sockets if the engine requires them)
Vise-Grips
8" to 12" pipe wrench
Crescent wrench
Impact wrench
Needlenose pliers
Side-cutting pliers
Slotted screwdrivers
Phillips screwdrivers
Ball peen hammer
Hacksaw and blades
Punches and chisels
Files
Feeler (thickness) gauges

Propane torch
Stainless steel threaded rod—1/4″, 3/8″, and 1/2″—plus a collection of nuts and washers

Engine Spares (this is an absolute bare minimum)

Oil and filters
Oil squirt can
Fuel filters
Belts
Oil filter wrench
Grease gun and grease
Water pump(s) impellers
WD 40 (lots of it!)
Gasket cement
Thermostat

Gasoline Engines (add to the above)

Spark plugs
Points and condenser
Distributor cap, rotor arm, and high-tension leads
Coil
Carburetor rebuild kit, including a carburetor float
Test light

"Leak" Kit

Underwater epoxy
Spare hoses
Stainless steel hose clamps
An inner tube
Duct tape
Fids for through hulls
One or two plywood blanks to fit all porthole sizes, together
    with some means of fastening them in place
Caps for all chimneys and Dorade vents
Spare companionway dropboards

Packing for stuffing boxes (packing glands)
Packing removal tool
Impellers, valves, and diaphragms for all pumps on board
Teflon tape
O-ring kit (a mixed assortment of O-rings)

Rigging and Steering Kit

At least one length of stainless steel wire as long as the longest
   stay on the boat
Norseman or Sta-Lok terminals for all wire sizes on the boat
Turnbuckles (rigging screws) for all wire sizes on the boat
Toggles for all wire sizes on the boat
Clevis pins
Cotter pins (cotter keys or split pins)
Cable clamps
Thimbles
Shackles
Blocks
Seizing wire
Bolt cutters
Nicopress kit (frequently Nicopress jaws can be bought to fit
   standard boltcutters)
A piece of lumber for spreader and tiller repairs
A complete chain and wire rope assembly for a wheel steering
   system

Electrical Kit

Electrician's tape
Heat shrink tape (available from Radio Shack)
Crimp-type wire terminals
Crimping tool
Wire
Wire stripper
Fuses and breakers
Multimeter

Soldering tips for the propane torch (in the mechanic's tool
   kit)
Solder and flux

Woodworking Tools

As considered necessary

Index